THIS
BOOK
BELONGS TO
Helen
+
Peter
Wigglesworth

The Romance of the

Grand Tour

100 years of Travel in South East Asia

The Romance of the
Grand
Tour

100 years of Travel in South East Asia

Kennie Ting

TALISMAN

Hongkong Harbour.

First published in 2015 by

Talisman Publishing Pte Ltd
52 Genting Lane #06-05
Ruby Land Complex 1
Singapore 349560
talisman@apdsing.com
www.talismanpublishing.com

ISBN 978-981-07-9604-4

Copyright © 2015 Talisman Publishing Pte Ltd

Text © Kennie Ting
Editor Kim Inglis
Creative Director Norreha Sayuti
Designers Foo Chee Ying, Stephy Chee
Studio Manager Janice Ng
Publisher Ian Pringle

Printed in Singapore

Contents

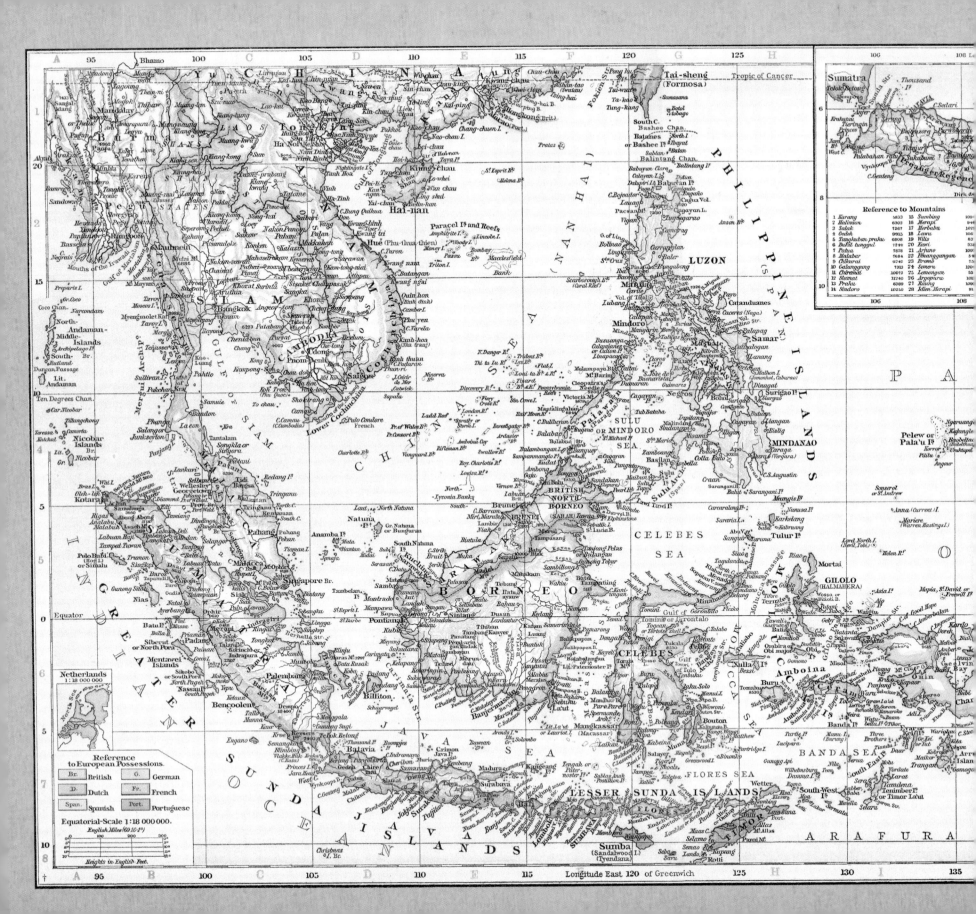

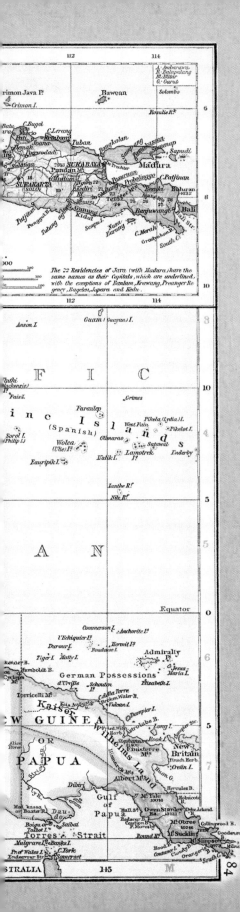

East of Suez

"Ship me somewheres east of Suez, where the best is like the worst,
Where there aren't no Ten Commandments an' a man can raise a thirst;
For the temple-bells are callin', an' it's there that I would be —
By the old Moulmein Pagoda, looking lazy at the sea."

— Rudyard Kipling, *Mandalay* (1892)

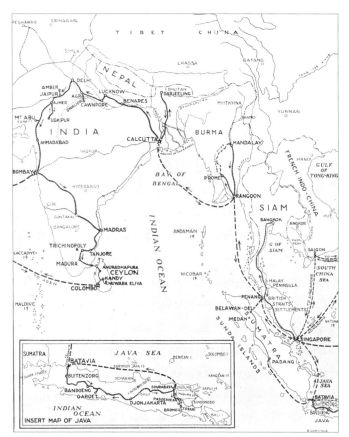

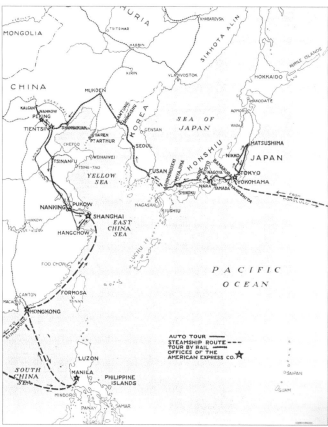

"East of Suez" — a phrase made popular by a poem published in 1892 by Rudyard Kipling, that doyen of all things Far Eastern — is what the European powers called their colonial dominions lying east of the Suez Canal. It is the subject of this book — most specifically a nostalgic journey through 12 port cities that stretched from Burma (today's Myanmar) to Hong Kong.

Before the opening of the Suez Canal in 1869, only colonial civil servants or merchants with an interest in far-flung foreign dominions travelled to the East. By and large, the traveller of leisure was few and far between, and had to be very intrepid to desire to take such a long and arduous journey. The opening of the Suez Canal by a Franco-Egyptian consortium in 1869 changed all that.

For the first time, ships heading east from Europe no longer needed to round the Cape of Good Hope and the entire African continent to get to Arabia, less than 2,000 miles from Greece. Months were shaved off the journey: this not only benefitted long-distance maritime trade, it proved pivotal in the development of long-distance leisure travel. Thus, by the 1880s, a small number of civilian travellers began to venture forth where no other of their time had been before — and return to recount their tales.

At the time, such travellers were exceptional passengers on board mail or cargo steamers. But, by the turn of the 19th century, pleasure cruises became a viable industry. Affluent Europeans, drawn by stories of the exotic Near and Far East, yearned to see the sights for themselves. The Great War (1914–1918) did little to quell demand, and by the 1920s, the cruise liner industry was at its peak. Thus, the Grand Tour of the East was born; and many a Grand Tourist embarked on the journey of a lifetime.

A few major shipping companies dominated this market. Most of them were considered "national" lines, much like the national airline carriers of today, and all invariably originated as mail carriers, conveying letters and parcels to and from Europe (and later America) to European colonies around the world. Originally plying the route between Europe and Asia, they later continued further east.

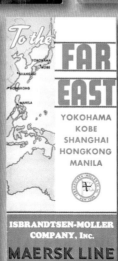

Above and opposite: *A selection of colourful brochures for the Grand Tour out East: Notable shipping companies that still exist include the British Peninsula & Oriental Steam Navigation Company (better known as P & O) and Cunard Line, the Danish Maersk Line and East Asiatic Company, and the Japanese Nippon Yusen Kaisha (NYK). They were all established in the 19th century, as were a bevy of other European companies that may not exist in their original form any more. Chief amongst these were the French Compagnie des Messageries Maritimes (literally "Maritime Packet Company"); the Dutch Koninklijke Paketvaart-Maatschappij (Royal Packet Navigation Company), or KPM; and the German Norddeutscher-Lloyd Line and Hamburg Amerikanische Paketfahrt Actien-Gesellschaft (Hamburg-America Line or HAPAG).*

Later, the development of the Pacific Route that plied from America to the East and onward to Europe saw the Americans getting in on the act. Their Dollar Steamship Company (1900) soon became very competitive with a fleet of large and luxurious "President Liners" by the 1920s.

In the 1920s, newly affluent Europeans and Americans seemed to have an insatiable curiosity to see a world they read about in journals and heard about in news' broadcasts. For them, the East presented a thrilling, albeit somewhat fantastical counterpoint to the West, with its social niceties, its modern conveniences and its increasingly hectic pace of life.

Of-the-era brochures from the major shipping lines, as well as independent tour agencies such as Thomas Cook & Son, Raymond & Whitcomb Company and American Express's travel department reinforced this impression of the East as an exotic and idyllic haven. The passage was described in terms of a return to innocence or, at least, to a simpler and more spiritual existence. Place names were exotic; cultures untamed. Mind-boggling distances and unfamiliar countries were rendered more manageable through detailed descriptions and evocative photographs that brought the locale to the would-be traveller.

In response to the increased demand for travel, the same shipping lines and tour agencies began to offer round-the-world cruises as early as the 1910s. Circumnavigating the globe, such tours catered to a select group of wealthy persons of leisure, or famous celebrities and writers. Often taking a whole year or more, itineraries included long stopovers at major ports, allowing the travellers to absorb the sights and experience the local histories and cultures.

There were two typical routes by which tourists travelled round the globe. The Suez Route commenced from the major European shipping headquarters — Southampton, Liverpool, Marseille, Amsterdam, Rotterdam, Bremen, Hamburg, Copenhagen, Trieste (Italy) and so on — and passed through the Suez Canal en route to the East. The ships berthed at a handful of cities in India, the East Indies and China before terminating in either of the treaty port cities of Kobe or Yokohama in Japan. Passengers on a round-the-world journey then transferred to a trans-Pacific liner onwards to North or South America.

For American liners, the journey was reversed and was known as the Pacific Route. Transatlantic liners would commence in the coastal port cities of Seattle, San Francisco or Los Angeles, and head west to get East (a somewhat ironic turn of events), terminating in Kobe or Yokohama, or equally often, Manila, in the American Philippines. Round-the-worlders then hopped onto another liner heading west, through the East Indies, India and Suez to Europe.

At the centre of the cruise liner industry was the steamship itself, which came in many different shapes and sizes, each with its own unique Arcadian name, like the M.S. Ophir, or the S.S. Britannia, or the R.M.S. Carpathia.

The abbreviations prefixing each name referred to the nature of the vessel. M.S. stood for "Motor Ship" and M.V. for "Motor Vessel," meaning the vessel was powered by an internal combustion engine that was fed with diesel. "S.S." stood for "Steam Ship", where the vessel was propelled by a steam engine. Occasionally, a ship would be prefixed with R.M.S. or "Royal Mail Ship," indicating that the ship was on contract with the British Royal Mail to carry mail abroad.

Most ships were medium-sized freighters built for the original purpose of conveying mail across long distances. These typically provided passage and accommodations for up to two dozen passengers in First Class staterooms, and continued to offer such passenger services up until World War II. Passenger liners were introduced in the early 1910s in response to demand for long-distance leisure travel. These were large-scale cruise ships that carried hundreds and even more than 1,000 passengers at a go, while also fulfilling a fundamental purpose as a mail ship.

Modes of transportation on round-the-world tours weren't limited to maritime steamships only. Tour agencies were committed to making the most of existing sea, river, land and, by the early 1920s, air travel networks in the region to transport such travellers.

The shipping lines were constantly competing with each other to offer the speediest, smoothest and most luxurious passages in the market. No cost and effort was spared in ensuring that the interior décor of these ships, particularly in First Class, was opulent, even decadent. In fact, many of the dining halls, lounges and smoking rooms were theatrical, reinforcing the impression that one was participating in a kind of sweeping epic drama.

Everyday life on board typically revolved around food and entertainment. The former was abundant, with the gong ringing all day long for breakfast, lunch, tea, supper and other light meals in between. Wine and beer was plentiful, and champagne was occasionally popped for First Class passengers. Guests dressed up outside of their private staterooms, in particular for dinner, where they joined other guests in the sumptuous dining rooms, to be treated to multi-course meals and resident musical ensembles. In between meals, social activity centered on the common spaces: open air promenade decks, the lounge halls and the smoking rooms, the latter restricted to First Class male passengers, who idled their time away on cards, drink and conversation, all the while puffing away on a cigar or cigarette.

Though never formally known as such, the "Grand Tour of the East" was inspired by a similar Grand Tour, that of Continental Europe, which began in the late 1700s and remained a popular rite of passage for wealthy élites in Britain and America well into the 1900s. Such a tour involved an exploration of classical antiquity and took in the major cultural capitals of the continent — Paris, Vienna, Milan, Venice, Florence, Rome, Athens — and terminated typically in Constantinople (Istanbul).

The Grand Tourist lingered at destinations for weeks or months at a time, touring ruins and attending artistic performances. Armed with letters of introduction to family connections, the goal was to return home better educated and better connected, politically and socially, thereby becoming a more valuable commodity in the job or marriage market.

The Eastern version of the tour was similar to the European, except the intent wasn't so much to better or educate one's self, but to experience something new and exotic; in other words, leisure, rather than self-advancement. There was also an undeniable degree of colonial superiority, with Westerners tending to objectify unfamiliar Eastern cultures and judge them as inferior to the West, rather than accept and attempt to understand them as equally viable alternatives.

The customary stops depended in large part on the colonial Empire from which the traveller hailed. Generally, the tour took in a handful of major port cities from India through the East Indies (as South East Asia was then called) to China and Japan. Those with time and money to spare would use these port cities as a base from which to take excursions to major historic sites and centres of culture — the palaces of Rajasthan, the ruins of Bagan, Angkor, Borobudur and Ayutthaya, the imperial cities of Beijing and Tokyo.

The East Indies was an important stopover between India and the Far East, not just because of its geographical location between the two. Rather, the East Indies was important because it was here, in this far-flung landscape of peninsulas and archipelagos that all of the major colonial European powers had significant territories and were thus represented. In other words, it was an extension of Europe (and America) itself, and its cities familiar re-creations of the imperial cities — London, Paris, Amsterdam — back home, offering respite to travellers in between the vast, alien and alienating expanses of India and China.

Top: A luggage label for Pan American (Pan Am) World Airways, 1930s/40s.
Opposite: Steamship memorabilia depicting sample round-the-world routes, fares and passages, floor-plans and life on board ship, 1910s–30s.

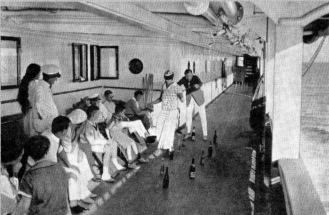

P A S S A G E S

TARIEF **FARES** **TARIF** **PREISE**

						ANTWERPEN																	
f 20		HAMBURG	f 15		f 95	f 105	£22	£22	£24	£28		£44	£60	£66	£72	£60	£60	£62	£64		£66	£66	£66	£66
f 45	f 15	ROTTERDAM		f 80	f 90	£20	£20	£22	£28		£40	£56	£62	£68	£56	£58	£60	£60		£62	£62	£62	£62
—	—	BARCELONA 1)	—	—	—	—	—	—	—		£54	—	—	£54	£54	£56	£58		£60	£60	£60	£60
—	—	MARSEILLE	f 10	£16	£16	£18	£22		£36	£52	£58	£64	£52	£52	£54	£56		£58	£58	£58	£58
f 115	f 105	f 90	GENUA	£15	£15	£17	£22		£36	£52	£58	£64	£52	£52	£54	£56		£58	£58	£58	£58
			JAFFA (HAIFA)	£2	£3	£20		£34	£42	£48	£54	£48	£51	£54	£54		£58	£58	£58	£58
£25	£22	£20	PORT SAID	£15	£2		£32	£40	£46	£52	£46	£49	£52	£54		£56	£56	£56	£56
£27	£24	£22	£17	SUEZ	£12		£32	£40	£46	£52	£46	£49	£52	£54		£56	£56	£56	£56
£34	£32	£28	£24	£15	£12	ADEN	£32	£30	£36	£42	£36	£39	£42	£44		£46	£46	£46	£46
£46	£44	£40	£36	£32	£32	£22	COLOMBO	£16	£22	£28	£18	£22	£24	£26		£29	£29	£29	£29
£62	£60	£56	£52	£40	£40	£30	£16	S'PORE/PENANG	£10	£12	£14	£14		£20	£20	£20	£20
£68	£66	£62	£58	£46	£46	£36		BANGKOK 2)									
£74	£72	£68	£64	£52	£52	£42		SAIGON 3)									
£62	£60	£56	£52	£46	£46	£36	£18	£10	MANILA 4)	H.$ 80	M.$ 95	M.$ 140	Y. 205	Y. 200	Y. 195	Y. 190
£62	£60	£56	£52	£49	£49	£39	£12	P. 50	HONGKONG	M.$ 50	M.$ 100	Y. 170	Y. 155	Y. 140	Y. 130
								FOOCHOW	M.$ 50		Y. 135	Y. 120	Y. 110	Y. 100
£66	£64	£60	£56	£54	£54	£44	£26	£14	P. 90	H.$ 90	SHANGHAI	Y. 105	Y. 95	Y. 85	Y. 70
£68	£66	£62	£58	£56	£56	£46	£29	£18	P. 120	H.$ 140	M.$ 60	DAIREN	
£68	£66	£62	£58	£56	£56	£46	£29	£20	P. 155	H.$ 180	M.$ 120	Y. 70	YOKOHAMA 5)
£68	£66	£62	£58	£56	£56	£46	£29	£20	P. 165	H.$ 190	M.$ 130	Y. 85	NAGOYA 5)
£68	£66	£62	£58	£56	£56	£46	£29	£20	P. 175	H.$ 195	M.$ 140	Y. 95	OSAKA 5)
£68	£66	£62	£58	£56	£56	£46	£29	£20	P. 180	H.$ 200	M.$ 150	Y. 105	KOBE 5)

¹) BARCELONA. In het tarief is begrepen 1e klasse passage van Marseille naar Barcelona. Alle overige kosten zijn voor rekening van de passagiers.

²) BANGKOK. In het tarief naar en van Bangkok zijn begrepen de kosten voor een passage- of spoorbiljet 1e klasse van Bangkok naar Singapore of Penang, resp. van Bangkok naar Singapore of Penang, tot een maximum van het 1e klasse B.I.-tarief op dit traject. Alle overige kosten zijn voor rekening van de passagiers.

³) SAIGON. Het tarief naar en van Saigon is inclusief vrije passage van Singapore naar Saigon of omgekeerd tot een maximum van het 2e klasse tarief der Messageries Maritimes. Alle overige kosten zijn voor rekening van de passagiers.

⁴) MANILA. Passagiers naar Manila betalen $8.- „head tax" extra.

⁵) JAPAN. Passagiers voor Japansche havens kunnen, desgewenscht, te Shanghai de reis voortzetten per mailboot. De kosten van het passagebiljet 1e klasse zijn voor rekening van de maatschappij.

¹) BARCELONA. Fares to Barcelona include a 1st class passage Marseilles — Barcelona by any line. All transhipment and/or other expenses are for passengers' account.

²) BANGKOK. Fares to and from Bangkok include 1st class steamer- or railticket Singapore — Bangkok, resp. Bangkok — Singapore or Penang not exceeding the 1st class B.I. fare Singapore — Bangkok or Bangkok — Singapore. All transhipment and/or other expenses are for passengers' account.

³) SAIGON. Fares to and from Saigon include a free passage by any line from Singapore to Saigon resp. from Saigon to Singapore not exceeding the 2nd M.M. Co. fare.

⁴) MANILA. Passengers to Manila pay $8.- head tax extra.

⁵) JAPAN. Passengers for Japanese ports have the option to continue the voyage from Shanghai by passengerliner. The cost of a 1st class ticket is for account of the Company.

¹) BARCELONE. Les tarifs pour Barcelone comprennent le billet de passage en 1ère classe de Marseille à Barcelone par une autre ligne. Tous les frais de transbordement et autres sont à la charge des passagers.

²) BANGKOK. Les tarifs et pour Bangkok comprennent le billet de 1ère classe (bateau ou chemin de fer) Singapour — Bangkok ou respectivement Bangkok — Singapour ou Penang, ne devant pas dépasser le prix en 1ère classe de la „B.I." Singapour — Bangkok ou Bangkok — Singapour. Tous frais de transbordement et autres sont à la charge des passagers.

³) SAIGON. Les tarifs de et pour Saigon comprennent un passage gratuit de Singapour à Saigon et respectivement de Saigon à Singapour ne devant pas dépasser le prix en 2ème classe des „M.M.".

⁴) MANILLE. Sur le tarif de passage pour Manille il sera perçu $8.- de „head tax" en supplément.

⁵) JAPON. Les passagers à destination des ports japonais auront la possibilité de continuer leur voyage de Shanghai par un paquebot. Le montant du billet de 1ère classe sera à la charge de la Compagnie.

¹) BARCELONA. Im Tarif ist eingeschlossen der Wert einer 1. Klasse Passage von Marseille nach Barcelona. Alle übrigen Kosten gehen zu Lasten der Passagiere.

²) BANGKOK. Im Tarif nach und von Bangkok sind die Kosten eingeschlossen für ein Passage- oder Eisenbahnbillet 1. Klasse von Singapore nach Bangkok bezw. von Bangkok nach Singapore oder Penang, zum Höchstbetrage des 1. Klasse B.I. Tarifs für diesen Dienst. Alle übrigen Kosten gehen zu Lasten der Passagiere.

³) SAIGON. Im Tarif nach und von Saigon ist eingeschlossen die freie Passage von Singapore nach Saigon oder umgekehrt zum Höchstbetrage des II. Klasse Tarifs der Messageries Maritimes. Alle übrigen Kosten gehen zu Lasten der Passagiere.

⁴) MANILA. Passagiere nach Manila haben $8.- amerikanische Kopfsteuer extra zu zahlen.

⁵) JAPAN. Fahrgäste für japanische Häfen können, falls erwünscht, die Reise von Shanghai mit einem Passagierschiff fortsetzen. Die Kosten der Passage I. Klasse gehen zu Lasten der Gesellschaft.

ROUTE OF THE WORLD TOUR

—— Route of "CASTLE" Vessels
—— Route of "TAI" Vessels

M.S. "Peter Maersk", M.S. "Anna Maersk": (Built 1932)

Deadweight: 8805 tons
Speed: about 15 knots
Number of Passengers: 14 in 7 double staterooms. 2 in single staterooms. Total: 16.
Bath facilities: Connecting shower bath with each double stateroom. Private shower bath with each single stateroom. Hot and cold running water in every stateroom. Separate tub bath on each passenger deck.

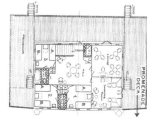

M/S PETER MAERSK and ANNA MAERSK

s. s. "Tasman"

5.023 TONS

FITTED WITH WIRELESS TELEGRAPHY

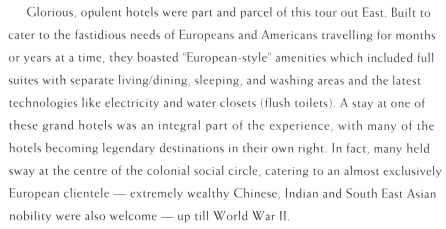

Glorious, opulent hotels were part and parcel of this tour out East. Built to cater to the fastidious needs of Europeans and Americans travelling for months or years at a time, they boasted "European-style" amenities which included full suites with separate living/dining, sleeping, and washing areas and the latest technologies like electricity and water closets (flush toilets). A stay at one of these grand hotels was an integral part of the experience, with many of the hotels becoming legendary destinations in their own right. In fact, many held sway at the centre of the colonial social circle, catering to an almost exclusively European clientele — extremely wealthy Chinese, Indian and South East Asian nobility were also welcome — up till World War II.

Every one of their guest-lists read like a veritable who's who of the most important persons of the time. Heads of state, royalty, *taipans* and business tycoons, socialites, celebrities and entertainers, even notorious gangsters and international criminals, all featured prominently within their rarefied walls.

Nonetheless, it would fall to the writers and poets to immortalise the gilded vision of life in these Far Eastern hotels: Somerset Maugham, George Orwell, Noel Coward, Rudyard Kipling and Joseph Conrad (to name but a few) in the Anglophone tradition; André Malraux, Pierre Loti and Marguerite Duras in the Francophone tradition; and

Louis Couperus, E. du Perron and Robert Nieuwenhuys in the Dutch tradition. Some of these writers had been born or lived significant parts of their lives in the Far East before repatriating to the West. Others undertook the Grand Tour and returned to tell the tale.

Thankfully, many of these grand hotels have somehow withstood the test of time and continue to stand today. Indeed, on this Grand Tour of South East Asia on which you, the readers, are about to embark, we pay a visit to a handful of them. Starting in Rangoon, we head south through the Straits of Malacca for the three Straits Settlements port towns of Georgetown (Penang), Malacca and Singapore, before heading to the Dutch East Indies, a dominion that extends for miles across a vast and shimmering ocean. After Batavia and Soerabaja, our ship heads north to drop anchor at Bangkok, the capital of Imperial Siam, the only territory in the East Indies not held by any colonial power. Afterwards, we head to French Indochina — from Saigon, the capital of Cochinchina, up the mighty Mekong River to Phnom Penh, then to the ancient citadel of Hanoi, the capital of Tonkin. From Tonkin, the ship wends itself east towards the Philippine Islands and its capital, Manila, before we reach our final destination and the gateway to the Far East proper: Hong Kong.

The Sarkies Brothers

Notable personalities linked to the grand hotels weren't limited to guests alone. The remarkable Sarkies brothers were associated with a good half a dozen legendary — including the most legendary — hotels in the East.

Originating from New Julfa, an Armenian enclave in the Persian city of Isfahan, each brother made his way to the region by way of British India. There were four brothers in total — Martin, the eldest, was the first to arrive in Malaya, but it was Tigran, the second brother, who possessed that entrepreneurial streak, co-founding with Martin in 1885, the company "Sarkies Brothers", and going on to establish first the Eastern & Oriental Hotel in Penang that same year, and then the Raffles Hotel in Singapore two years later. Aviet, the third brother, established the Strand Hotel in Rangoon in 1901, after a string of other entrepreneurial ventures. Meanwhile, the youngest brother, Arshak, took over the management reins of the E & O, becoming the brother most indelibly linked to that establishment.

By the early 1900s, the Sarkies Brothers were the leading hoteliers in the East, counting, amongst their properties, not just the Raffles, the E & O and the Strand, but also the Crag Hotel in Penang, as well as the Seaview Hotel and the Raffles Tiffin Room in Singapore. A cousin managed the nearby Adelphi Hotel in Singapore, while a Javanese branch of the Sarkies family, headed by Martin's son, Lucas Martin Sarkies, went on to helm the fabled Hotel Oranje in the port city of Soerabaja.

Sadly, the main Malayan branch of the Brothers went bankrupt in 1931, in the thick of the Great Depression and following Arshak Sarkies' tragic and untimely death of a heart attack in the E & O. From thence, management of all their hotels passed out of the family's hands, with the exception of the Oranje, which continued to be managed by Lucas Martin and his descendants until the 1960s.

SARKIES' HOTELS

RAFFLES HOTEL,
SINGAPORE.
Telegrams : " Raffles, Singapore."

STRAND HOTEL,
RANGOON.
Telegrams : " Sarkies, Rangoon."

E. & O. HOTEL,
PENANG.
Telegrams : " Sarkies, Penang."

THE CRAG HOTEL,
PENANG HILLS.
Telegrams : " Sarkies, Penang."

The headquarters of Mr. Frank C. Clarks',
Tourists in Burmah and Straits Settlements.

SARKIES BROTHERS,
PROPRIETORS.

Opposite, left: Luggage label for the Raffles Hotel in Singapore, 1950s.
Opposite, right: An image of the Galle Face Hotel in Colombo in what was then Ceylon.
Far left, from left to right: Joe Constantine, manager of the Raffles Hotel, Arshak Sarkies, Martin Sarkies, and Martyrose Arathoon (to manage the Adelphi Hotel later on). Constantine and Arathoon were fellow Armenians.
Left: Advertisement for Sarkies' Hotels, from a 1909 travel brochure for Burma.

Above: Our Grand Tour takes us to 12 cities in present-day South East Asia and some of the region's most historic sights are pictured here. **Clockwise from top left:** The Shwedagon Pagoda in Rangoon; Penang's famous Blue Mansion; Christchurch in Malacca; the Singapore waterfront; the former Dutch Stadhuis in Batavia (today's Jakarta); the Red Bridge in Soerabaja; the Grand Palace in Bangkok; Ha Long Bay and junk in French Indochina (Vietnam); Angkor Wat in Cambodia; Hanoi's Hoan Kiem Lake; the Rizal Monument in Manila, and finally, Hong Kong's iconic Victoria Harbour.

Rangoon (Yangon)

"Sometimes I think that in two hundred years all this — "
he waved a foot towards the horizon — "all this will be gone
— forests, villages, monasteries, pagodas all vanished."

— George Orwell, *Burmese Days* (1934)

Previous page: *Bird's eye view of Strand Road and the Rangoon River in the 1920s.*
Above: *Bird's eye view over downtown Rangoon towards the Sule Pagoda, also from the same period.*
Opposite, left to right: *1890s view of Rangoon landing stage with a steamship at berth, photograph of a high street in Rangoon, with the Rangoon High Court and Rangoon City Hall, 1890s; map of Burma from a 1903 publication, Ledger and Sword, or The honourable company of merchants of England trading to the East Indies (1599–1874).*

The Empire's Gateway to the East

Today, Yangon hasn't changed a great deal since the heady days of the British Empire, when it was known as Rangoon. One of the finest port cities east of Suez, it was a gateway city — the threshold between India and the Far East proper. From here on, China beckoned in all its exotic, glittering splendour; and beyond that, the hermit kingdom of Japan.

In 1852, in the aftermath of the Second Anglo-Burmese War, the British captured Rangoon and all of Lower Burma. Her Majesty's ever-enterprising subjects created a brand new city on a thoroughly rational grid plan by the banks of the Yangon River, and they transformed this once sleepy fishing settlement into a thriving hub for international trade and commerce. Rangoon became the furthestmost point of the British Raj (or British India) in 1886, when the rest of Burma capitulated and the province of British Burma was formed.

As the commercial and political capital of British Burma, Rangoon received considerable investment into infrastructure and urban planning. The city became known for its broad tree-lined boulevards flanked by monumental civic and commercial buildings; its row after row of lily-white colonial bungalows in its expansive military cantonment and residential suburbs; and for the many idyllic lakes and parks that fell within its limits.

For almost a century, Rangoon fulfilled its role as the showpiece city of British imperial munificence. In all aspects it was the "London of the East" — it had public transport,

Left: *The Accountant General's Office (1912), still standing today.*
Top: *Photograph of Rangoon City Hall and the Sule Pagoda, 1930s.*
Above: *Photograph of elephants in Burma by Philip Adolphe Klier (P. Klier), 1890s.*
Below left: *Portrait of Aung San, the Father of modern-day Burma.*
Opposite: *Map of Rangoon clearly showing neat grid system, 1924.*

infrastructure and public services that were comparable to London; a quality of life that quite possibly surpassed the latter, due to the privileged status and luxurious lifestyles afforded to colonials; and a generally well-planned and beautifully landscaped city with monumental colonial architecture.

However, over time, this outward semblance of imperial control belied a growing wave of dissent amidst the Burmese, as Rangoon (called Yangon by the locals) became the centre of the Burmese independence movement. From the 1920s till the outbreak of World War II, there were nation-wide protests against British Rule, led by students of Rangoon University and in particular, one Aung San, who would go on to shepherd Burma towards formal independence. Sadly, he was assassinated by political rivals just six months before Burma attained independence in 1948.

A decade of ill-advised economic policies led to a 1962 *coup d'état* by the Burmese military and the country has been under military rule ever since. More recently, however, the country seems again on the brink of change and the Burmese are seeing improvements politically and economically.

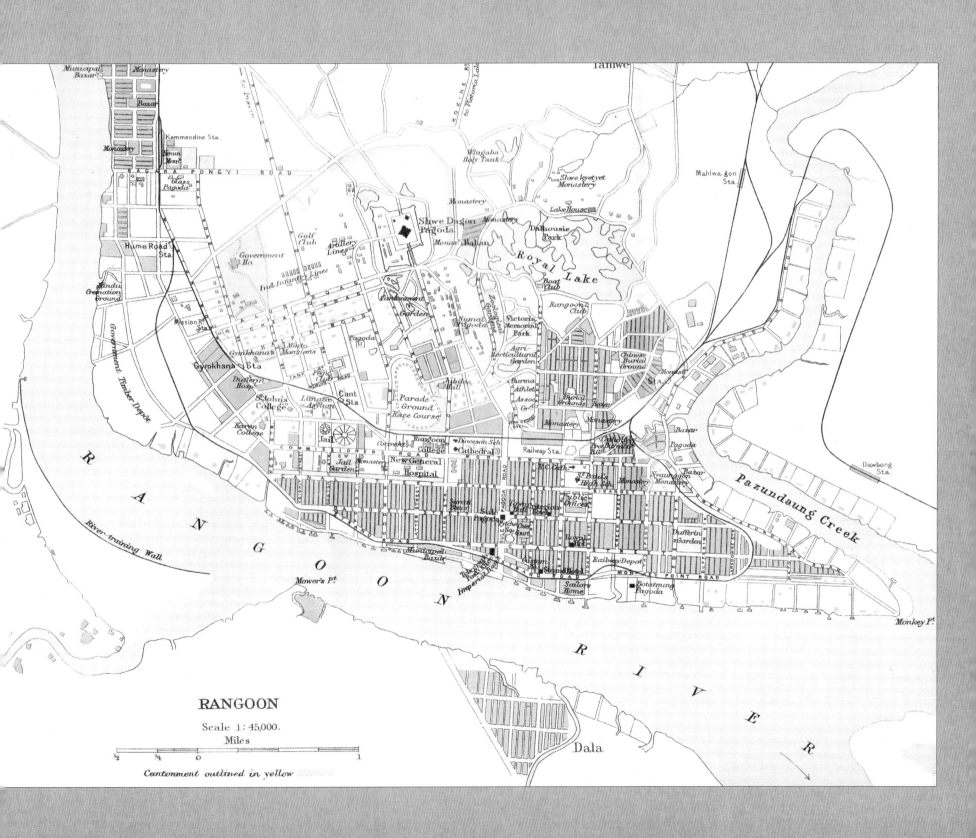

RANGOON

Scale 1 : 45,000.

Miles

Cantonment outlined in yellow

The British in Burma

Life in Rangoon typified "the colonial life": English *sahibs* — merchants, militarymen and colonial officials — lived, with their wives and children, in all-white suburban bungalows with green shutters and large verandahs, many of which still exist today and can be seen in the suburbs of Ahlone and Shwedagon. The household consisted of a retinue of Indian and Burmese staff who did the cooking and the cleaning, as well as *ayahs*, or nannies, who took care of the young ones.

The day began early, on account of the tropical heat, and lasted long. The menfolk went to the office in the early hours of the morning and did not leave till dusk. Tiffin was delivered to the workplace. When evening finally fell, and the temperature dropped slightly, the men emerged from their offices for a drink at the club or to join their wives for dinner parties and other social engagements, or to take leisurely strolls along the tree-lined avenues and by the lake in fashionable Dalhousie Park (today's Bogyoke Aung San Park).

As in other cities of the British Empire, the club was the centre of the social scene, particularly for the men. Rangoon boasted a few including the Gymkhana Club, more of a sports club offering cricket, tennis and other activities, and the Pegu Club (1882), a gentlemen's club, where Kipling was famously inspired to pen his poem *Mandalay*, and where the

Top: Colonial residence and horse-drawn carriage in present-day Maymyo.
***Above:** Burmese sahibs gathered round an automobile, 1913.*
***Right:** Portrait of Rudyard Kipling.*

sahibs would stop off for gin slings and boisterous conversation before retiring home for the evening. The former club has been demolished but the latter still stands today, albeit abandoned and in a decrepit state.

During the hot and humid summer months from June to September, trips were taken up country to the former royal capital of Mandalay, via the doughty steamships of the Irrawaddy Flotilla Company; or, more often than not, to the hill-station resort of Maymyo (today's Pyin U Lwin), accessible by Burmese Rail. There, the Governor had his summer residence, and many other colonials maintained estates reminiscent of stately residences or homely cottages in the Scottish Highlands. Today, Maymyo still boasts the largest population of Anglo-Burmese — descendants of the English colonials — and much of its colonial architecture is still intact.

Opposite, clockwise from top left: The Boat Club on Royal Lake, Rangoon; the Pegu Club, Rangoon; the Royal Palace, Mandalay; the Gymkhana, Rangoon; photograph of a steamship from the Irawaddy Flotilla Company, early 1900s.

Colonial Splendour

Above: *The Bank of Bengal Building (1914).*
Right, left to right: *Rangoon City Hall; the offices of Bulloch Brothers & Co. (1920s), presently a post office.*

Ironically, because modern-day, military junta-ruled Yangon was starved of foreign investment for much of the late 1900s, most of the city's colonial-era architecture still stands intact. This being so, visiting Yangon today feels very much like travelling back in time.

The most vivid expression of the city's glorious past is to be found downtown. The city here is an open-air museum — an ode to the brick, mortar and cast iron of Empire. Even though the British were in Burma for just under a century (1852–1948), they inscribed into the urban fabric some of their most over-the-top pieces of imperial architecture east of the Indian Subcontinent.

The colonial old town is concentrated east of the Sule Pagoda, one of Yangon's oldest Buddhist temples. Along Strand and Phayre (presently Pansoedan) Roads near the waterfront sit some of the most spectacular monuments, channelling other major port cities of the British Empire, notably Calcutta and Shanghai. Many of them still retain their names on the façades — "Rander House"; "Ascott & Co.", "Government Telegraph Office" — evoking a time when Rangoon, together with Singapore, was the most important hub for international trade and commerce in South East Asia.

The plethora of architectural styles in the old town is exhilaratingly diverse, ranging from exuberant Edwardian, to Oriental Italianate, to functional Art Deco. Italianate and, later, Art Deco, were the styles of choice of the many mercantile organisations and banks, and as such, Merchant and Bank Roads are where one finds some of the most impressive instances of these architectural vernaculars. In all instances, what is most likely to strike the visitor, however, is how alive these buildings are even though they are in a desperate state of repair.

This page: Examples of Edwardian architectural style include the imposing High Court Building (1914) in Yangon's central square (see postcard left below; it still stands today) and the ominous Secretariat Building, where Bogyoke (General) Aung San, the father of modern Burma, was assassinated in 1947. His daughter, Aung San Suu Kyi, continues his legacy of fighting for a modern-day democratic Burma.

At top there is a view of buildings on Strand Road from the late 1800s when it was a somnolent and laidback dirt road with horse carriages and sepoys; it is inset with a contemporary photograph of the New Law Courts Building (1927), built from the same stone.

Trade, Markets and More

Colonial Rangoon was a centre of trade and commerce, bringing goods and services from all over the world to Burma and exporting essential raw materials in return. The mercantile history of the city is written on to the face of the Old Town's urban landscape, with a wealth of architectural styles – cast iron, Art Deco, Beaux-Arts, (Chinese) shophouse — housing thousands of small and medium-sized businesses, largely family-owned and operated.

The city is no less entrepreneurial today than it was in colonial times. From the epicentre that is Bogyoke Market (1926), formally known as Scott's Market, the commercial quarter fans out in all directions and is surprisingly bustling and boisterous, proving that military rule from the '60s to the '00s, and years of corresponding economic sanctions by the international community, have not tarnished the entrepreneurial spirit of a hardy population.

Left: Bogyoke Market, the city's most famous marketplace.
Right, top to bottom: *A contemporary shopping mall in the city; the historic Thein Gyi Market (1905) which still sells traditional Burmese produce, foodstuff and wares today; the historic Rowe & Co. building (1911), once Rangoon's foremost department store and still extant today.*

Above left: *Thein Gyi market, 1890s.*
Above right: *Burmese street food seller.*
Left: *Advertisements from the early 1900s for Whiteaway, Laidlaw & Co. Ltd and Rowe & Co. Ltd – two major department stores in Rangoon and other British colonial port cities in the region.*

A Colourful Melting Pot

West of the Sule Pagoda sit the city's ethnic quarters — its Chinatown, Little India and Arab areas. Upon inception, Rangoon was indistinguishable from many of the colonial and treaty port cities that dotted maritime South East and East Asia. In other words, it was largely a foreign city in its own hinterland: for many years the Burmese were a minority in a cosmopolitan, multi-ethnic and multi-religious urban fabric.

Yangon's ethnic quarters still bear witness to this rich cultural and religious diversity. Here, the intrepid wanderer may find, secreted like hidden gems in the orderly British-imposed grid, more than a dozen different places of worship, representing all the major religions of the world. On adjacent blocks, there are Burmese, Chinese and Hindu temples, Anglican and Catholic churches, Sunni and Shi'a mosques, a Jewish synagogue and even an Ismaili *khanaqah*. Most of these are still active, and sit alongside the shophouses and apartment buildings from the early 1900s that still house bustling communities, living as they did more than a century ago.

The faces of these people are similarly multi-hued, with south Indians of both Hindu and Muslim persuasion being the most obvious minority group. The Chinese, hailing from the southern provinces of Fukien and Canton, often look largely indistinguishable from the Burmese themselves. However, the most populous ethnic group in the city today are the Burmese — they have successfully re-colonised the city from their erstwhile colonial masters.

Left top: St. Mary's Cathedral (1899).
Left bottom: Masjid Mogul Shiah (1914).
Above left: Entrance and carved stone tower to one of the many Hindu temples in the old town.
Above right: Imposing interior of Musmeah Yeshua Synagogue (1896).

Shwedagon Pagoda

Buddhism remains at the heart of Burmese culture and identity. The Buddhism practiced here is Theravada Buddhism which originated from Ceylon (today's Sri Lanka) and is infused with traces of Hindu Brahmanism, stressing a hierarchical and ordered structure to religion and society. The Burmese national symbol — the magnificent and surreal Shwedagon Pagoda — sees the usual array of Buddhist icons placed alongside statues of celestial beings and mythical beasts from the *Yama Zatdaw,* the Burmese incarnation of the Hindu epic, the *Ramayana.*

The tenets of Theravada Buddhism run deep in everyday Burmese life. Civilians far outnumber monks worshipping at the pagoda and many a matronly figure may be observed cultivating *karma* by slipping alms to silently waiting monks, sitting or standing amidst a forest of smaller pagodas and pavilion-temples that dot the sacred complex.

The most intriguing practice has to be the ritual washing of the Buddha: during this, ordinary citizens of all ages and backgrounds step up in an orderly manner to the dozen or so strategically placed white statues of Buddha set around the central pagoda, and proceed to douse the statue with cup after cup of holy water. Before them, dozens of devotees prostrate themselves, muttering benedictions as they wait their turn.

> *"An agreeable life, luncheon at this club or that, drives along trim, wide roads, bridge after dark at that club or this, gin pahits ... and then back through the night to dress for dinner and then out again to dine with this hospitable host or the other...."*
>
> — Somerset Maugham, *The Gentleman in the Parlour* (1931)

Above: *Advertisement extolling the services of the Strand Hotel, Rangoon, 1900s.*
Right: *Two different styles of luggage label from the Strand Hotel.*

The Strand Hotel

Opened in 1901, the Strand Hotel is the third and last extant property established by the Sarkies' Brothers, the illustrious Armenian family of hoteliers who helmed the most famous grand hotels in South East Asia. It was the brainchild of Aviet Sarkies, the youngest of the brothers, and his older brother Tigran, who had established the Raffles Hotel in Singapore 14 years earlier. However, it was the shortest-lived of the Sarkies' hotels, only remaining in the brothers' possession for 24 years — they sold it to a fellow Armenian businessman in 1925.

In the early 1900s, the Strand sat across a small road from a large waterfront park on the banks of the Rangoon River, near the port of Rangoon. Today, this road — Strand Road — is a huge and busy multi-lane thoroughfare lined with almost a dozen of the most impressive colonial-era buildings in the city, strongly recalling the Shanghai Bund.

In the days of the British Raj, British tourists alighted from their luxury cruise liner that had departed from Calcutta some three days previously to a familiar and edifying sight — a pompous display of the wealth, might and power of the Empire. Then it was a short walk from the jetty in front of the hotel to the Strand's entranceway, where a waiting Sikh footman ushered them in (today he has been replaced by a Burmese footman in traditional *longyi*).

Once inside, the traveller was surrounded by a delightful, otherworldly paradise of potted palms, expansive marble floors, wicker chairs and leisurely flapping *punkahs* — large cloth fans hung from the ceiling and pulled upon by *punkah wallahs*, Indian servants whose sole employment it was to keep the air cool and circulating. The ambience was convivial: a reassuring buzz of activity and the symphony of (mainly English) voices.

Above: *The Strand Hotel, by P. Klier. Photographic print, 1895.*
Right: *The Strand Hotel today, with the Rangoon Port Trust Commission Building (1920) in the background.*

These would have come from fellow guests having afternoon tea in the lobby lounge or gin *pahits* in the hotel bar. Ensconced in the corner of the lobby, a novelist or journalist may have been taking notes whilst smoking a cigar; elsewhere, local colonials escaping the office lounged in the tropical garb of topee, short-sleeved shirts and neatly starched shorts.

Left and opposite: Interior views of the Strand Hotel, including guest accommodations, the Strand Bar and the famous Lobby Lounge. A complete renovation of the hotel has resulted in a major facelift, but the atmosphere of old remains.
Below: A portrait of George Orwell.

Naturally, service was close to impeccable with our Grand Tourist being whisked up to his suite in a matter of minutes, followed by his entourage of boxes, trunks and manservants. Once settled in, he was ready to commence his month- or even year-long residence in this home away from home.

Burmese Days — A Savage Indictment of Colonialism

George Orwell was posted to Lower Burma between 1922 and 1927. He was a police officer in the Indian Imperial Police Force — in those days, Lower Burma was governed as a part of the British Raj in India. There, he was appalled by British colonial society, in particular by the stultifying aimlessness and rampant racism he saw all around him. He would later pen his observations into a best-selling novel, *Burmese Days*, published in 1934 and still regarded today as one of the most compelling pieces of colonial literature. It is rather likely that he penned some of these observations while at the Strand Hotel. It was certainly operating during his time and the hotel itself claims him as a guest.

Georgetown (Penang)

2

"Neither the mainland nor the adjacent islands attracted any interest in this country till the East India Company acquired Pinang in 1775, Province Wellesley in 1798, Singapore in 1823, and Malacca in 1824. These small but important colonies were consolidated in 1867 into one Government under the Crown, and are now known as the Straits Settlements, and prized as among the most valuable of our possessions in the Far East."

— Isabella Bird, *The Golden Chersonese and the Way Thither* (1883)

Straits Splendour

Previous page: *Georgetown waterfront in the 1920s with the Federated Malay States Railway Building (1907).*
Above: *Memorial to James Richardson Logan (1869), Light Street.*
Opposite below, left to right: *Government Offices and Victoria Clock Tower; two views of Georgetown harbour.*

In 1786, Captain Francis Light of the English East India Company landed on the island of Penang and claimed it for the Prince of Wales (the future George III). Politically part of the Malay Sultanate of Kedah, the island was formally ceded to the company only four years later in 1790, following a failed attempt by the Sultan to reclaim the island. The terms of the cessation included an annual sum of 6,000 Spanish dollars, to be paid in perpetuity — and still paid today by the State of Pinang to the Sultan.

The acquisition of Penang marked the beginning of a century and a half of British colonialism in the region — Burma, the rest of Malaya and North Borneo would come later. For a good half a century, Penang, blessed by its deep harbour and prime location on the Straits of Malacca, was a safe stopover for merchant ships of the British Empire plying the China trade, and it gained considerable prosperity. In the early 1800s, a plan was hatched to further enhance its infrastructure and convert it into a major naval depot and commercial hub, but then Raffles founded Singapore in 1819 — and Penang was passed over.

1824 saw the signing of the Anglo-Dutch Treaty, which divided the Malay Archipelago into the British and Dutch

colonial spheres of influence — a division that still exists today in the very arbitrary distinction between Malaysia (Brunei and Singapore) and Indonesia. Under the terms of the treaty, the Dutch colony of Malacca on the Malayan Peninsula was ceded to the British in exchange for the British colony of Bencoolen in Sumatra.

Penang, Singapore and Malacca were then grouped and governed together as a single colonial territory known as the Straits Settlements, with its capital based in Georgetown. This territory remained a separate entity from British Malaya up until 1946. In 1832, the capital of the Straits Settlements was shifted southwards from Penang to Singapore after the colonial authorities decided that Singapore's far better harbour and geographical position would make it the most superior and profitable port colony in the East.

Penang didn't simply close shop, however. It continued to thrive and prosper, and it is still one of the most bustling and multi-cultural cities in the East today. It watches its brash cousin down south closely but never emulates, and as such it retains a character quite distinct from Singapore and Malaysia itself.

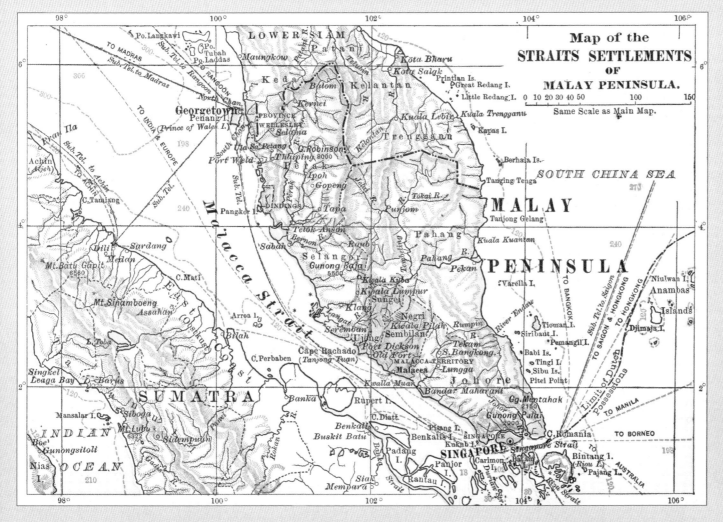

Map of the STRAITS SETTLEMENTS OF MALAY PENINSULA.

0 10 20 30 40 50   100   150

Same Scale as Main Map.

Map of the Straits Settlements

The Straits Settlements, as originally constituted, consisted of Penang, Malacca and Singapore, three territories on the west coast of Malaya. They were ruled as part of British India until 1867, when they became a Crown Colony, answering directly to the British Colonial Office in London. The Dindings, consisting of some islands near the mouth of the Perak River and a small piece of territory on the adjoining mainland, were briefly included from 1874 to 1934. So was Labuan, an island off North Borneo, in 1906. The colony was dissolved in 1946 after World War II ended, with Penang and Malacca joining the Union of Malaya and Singapore becoming a Crown Colony.

Colonial Georgetown

Georgetown, the capital of Penang, located in the northeastern corner of the island, is one of the best-preserved British colonial cities in South East Asia. From the late 18th century up until World War II, it was the centre of trade and commerce on the island, housing the local offices of the Hong Kong & Shanghai Bank, the Chartered Bank of India, China and Australia, Guthrie & Co. and other international financial institutions and shipping companies; alongside colonial municipal offices. The resident European community lived largely in the vicinity of Georgetown, residing in bungalows in the outskirts of town and commuting into the bustling city centre for work.

Social life revolved around the numerous clubs and venues in the city. In the late afternoons, the men often popped out for a spot of cricket at the prestigious Penang Cricket Club, situated on a prime location on the eastern side of the Padang or public square. Early evenings saw married couples attending amateur or professional theatricals at the misleadingly named Town Hall, on the western side of the Padang; or cradling gin *pahits* and listening to the resident musical ensemble on the lawn of the Eastern & Oriental Hotel.

As Penang was usually the first stop for all ships passing through the Malacca Straits to the East Indies, it saw a regular flow of merchants, businessmen, tourists and new residents. The arrival of a mail steamer was always an event since more often than not it would bring an addition to the community — a blushing bride from the home countries, perhaps; or a bright-eyed and bushy-tailed young accountant eager to start his career in the East. Today, delightfully, Penang is easily taken in on foot. The length of the inner city can be traversed in no more than half an hour, though the reality is that the walk takes all day as one stumbles upon colonial-era civic buildings, period shophouses, temples, churches and mosques at every street corner. It's a fascinating history lesson at every turn.

Opposite: *Fort Cornwallis and the Victoria Clock Tower, presented in 1902 to Penang by the Honorable Cheah Chen Eok Esq, to commemorate Her Majesty Queen Victoria's Diamond Jubilee.*
Left: *View of Light Street in colonial times.*
Top: *Georgetown branch of the Hongkong & Shanghai Bank Corporation (1906).*
Above: *The Penang Cricket Club (1910).*

PENANG
Scale 1:30,000
English Mile
Kilometer

Map of Georgetown

The city of Georgetown is huddled at the northeastern corner of Penang Island, at the very tip of a triangular peninsula. This map, taken from the pages of a 1917 guidebook, shows the various streets in detail. The major colonial-era monuments are along Light Street and Beach Street, to the north and east of the peninsula – Fort Cornwallis is visible at top left, as are the Padang, just beside it, and the Esplanade.

Just behind these thoroughfares is Penang's multi-cultural core, spread along dozens of streets that echo the races that inhabit them — China Street, Chulia Street, Armenian Street, Acheen Street, and so on. To the north west of the Peninsula sits the prestigious Penang Club, and the grounds of the Eastern & Oriental Hotel. Ferry terminals to the mainland and beyond are at the north east. Georgetown's main ferry terminal is the Swettenham Pier, at far right, while the Federated Malay States Railway Station stands where it is marked "Railway Jetty".

Above: Views of Beach Street in the 1920s and the same street today.
Right: Map of Georgetown, 1917.

The European heart of the town occupies the northern and eastern shores of the inner city, where the Padang sits surrounded by a string of monumental civic, educational and cultural institutions. All the buildings have been so well preserved that they continue to exude a period atmosphere.

The same feeling of being deliciously out of time and place can be felt while cruising down Beach Street or *Lebuh Pantai* in a taxi. One fancies oneself a colonial-era tin or rubber magnate, fresh from a journey by train from Ipoh or Kuala Lumpur, on one's way to trade futures at one of the city's many reputable commercial institutions occupying a severe, Palladian-style building along the waterfront.

The main impression one gets from all this concentrated monumental posturing is one of imperial largesse. The British drew their ambitions into the urban planning and design of

Above: Penang Town Hall (1880) in the early 1900s and today, on left.
Below: The Anglican Church of St. George (1818) in the early 1900s and today.

Penang, which they then replicated on a much grander scale in Singapore — and elsewhere. In both cities, there are variations on the same Padang, the same Esplanade, the same Fort (Fort Cornwallis in Penang, the oldest British fort in Malaya), the same commercial and bank buildings, and even the same Beach Street (called Beach Road in Singapore).

The similarity in the urban landscaping between the two cities is usually overlooked today. This is particularly so in Singapore, where a towering, aspirational fabric often replaces and obscures the original colonial urban plan. One thing's for certain though: the form of both cities may have diverged, but their origins remain the same.

The Chinese in Penang

Penang, like many other South East Asian cities, is multi-ethnic and multi-religious. The most predominant ethnic group on the island is the Chinese, who have a long and deep-rooted presence in the city. There are three "tribes" of Chinese here, differentiated primarily by period of arrival in what was known as the Nanyang (or Southern Seas) region.

The first are the Peranakan, or Straits Chinese, descendants of sea-faring Chinese who emigrated to the Malay Archipelago in the 14th century, along with the fabled treasure fleets of Admiral Cheng Ho. Having inter-married across the centuries with indigenous Malays, Javanese, Siamese and Burmese, they evolved a kind of hybrid culture and language that mixed Chinese and Malay traditions. Many became fabulously wealthy, as evidenced in the stunning and marvelously preserved Pinang Peranakan Mansion, once a private residence.

The second group comprises the latter-day Chinese, those who arrived in the 1800s and 1900s from provinces in Southern China and who spoke a variety of Southern Chinese dialects: Hokkien, Cantonese, Teochew, Hakka, Hainanese, to name a few. Many arrived penniless with the hope of making their fortunes in South East Asia, and some became extremely prosperous and powerful. They left their mark on the city in the form of magnificent temples and private residences such as the Khoo Kongsi Temple Complex and the Cheong Fatt Tze or Blue Mansion (see page 47); and the many two-storeyed commercial shophouses with their five-foot ways, to be found throughout Georgetown (see opposite).

Finally, there are the water-based Chinese of Penang's Clan Jetties — evidenced by those out-of-this-world communities-on-stilts along the waterfront (see below). They comprise the remains of a vast expanse of such settlements that once colonised the coasts of most of East Asia's port cities, including Canton, Amoy, Saigon, Bangkok, Phnom Penh and even Singapore. Descendants of fisher-folk primarily from Fujian province, they are quite possibly the last of their kind today.

Above: *A Chinese junk, with its beautiful sails unfurled, in waters around Penang.*
Right top: *Portrait of a Straits Chinese lady taken by Nikko Studio, Penang, early 1900s.*
Right below: *Fishing boats along the Chew Clan Jetty, home to a fishing community that originated from Fujian province in China.*

Above: *Views of shophouses in the early 1900s and today, little has changed to the basic architectural form.*

Exploring Chinatown

Exploring Chinese heritage in downtown Penang is an absolute pleasure, particularly since there is so much of it remaining. Strolling down the many streets and side alleys of Georgetown, one is pleasantly charmed by the façades painted in pastel shades and the stone pillars carved with flora and fauna; by the quaint temples and miniature shrines that appear out of nowhere and are dedicated to a pantheon of different colourful deities; and by the ubiquitous scent of food — a unique combination of Chinese ingredients and Malay spices.

Naturally, one of the highlights of such a tour is the sight of the many rows of traditional Chinese shophouses. Their origins, derived from the Chinese courtyard house form, are mercantile — a remarkably efficient and elegant architecture that enabled migrant Chinese merchants to operate family businesses on the ground floor while maintaining residential apartments on the second. Eventually, some of these shophouses evolved to become entirely residential.

Deceptively small from the outside, shophouses extend deep within, and often have airwells and internal courtyards that provide air circulation and natural light. Another unique feature are the five-foot ways or recessed, sheltered pedestrian walkways on the ground floor, so-called due to their being supposedly five feet in width. These walkways were multi-functional: They protected from sun and rain; they allowed for cargo to be loaded and unloaded; they encouraged passers-by to stop, admire and purchase displayed goods; and most importantly, they facilitated communal interaction between the residents, merchants and passers-by.

Many Chinese in Malaysia and Singapore today have fond memories of these narrow theatres of everyday life — and luckily for the architecture enthusiast many have been well preserved in Penang.

UNESCO Recognition

In 2008, along with Malacca, Georgetown was recognised by UNESCO as a World Cultural Heritage site, an exemplary multi-cultural trading town with many layers of history. In particular, emphasis was placed on it being a showcase of living heritage, embodied not just in the continued use of many heritage buildings, but also in the observance of a variety of traditional customs practiced by the various ethnicities that share the city.

Jalan Masjid Kapitan Keling, known as Pitt Street in colonial times and called Penang's "Street of Harmony" today, houses a number of the city's most significant Chinese temples, Hindu temples and Muslim mosques, often standing side by side as a physical statement of the city's tolerance and diversity. During important festivals, such as the Chinese Lunar New Year, the Muslim Hari Raya Puasa or the Hindu Thaipusam, the streets are enlivened as the respective ethnic communities undertake processions in celebration of their culture and heritage. These are times when Penang comes truly alive.

In addition, there are a number of protected buildings, some of which have been meticulously restored, more often than not by private individuals. Of particular note are the Khoo Kongsi Clan and Temple Complex (1835) and the Blue Mansion, the latter located on Leith Street (see opposite).

Opposite, top far left: *Photograph of Kapitan Keling Mosque on Pitt Street, 1930s.*
Opposite, bottom far left: *Portrait of a Sepoy, an early resident of Penang, 1880s.*
Opposite right, clockwise from top left: *The Penang Islamic Museum; devotee in the Hindu festival of Thaipusam; the Goddess of Mercy Temple (1728) on Pitt Street.*
Above: *A traditional Chinese opera performance.*

This page: *The Blue Mansion, built in the 1880s by a wealthy Chinese merchant, Cheong Fatt Tze, is a unique East meets West combination. The style is that of a traditional Chinese courtyard house, but the floor tiles come from Stoke-on-Trent and the cast iron stairwork was shipped over from Glasgow. That notwithstanding, the dwelling was built to strict feng shui principles — its back faces a hill and it sports an internal courtyard, airwell and drainage system that allows for rainwater to flow continuously inside the house.*

Painstakingly restored in the late 1990s, it was recognised by UNESCO in 2000 with a "Most Excellent" Heritage Conservation Award. Today, it is a luxury bed and breakfast popular with the heritage enthusiast. Unfortunately, it stands surrounded by contemporary high-rise developments that erode much of the period feel that must have pervaded through the mansion in the past.

Outside the City Centre

No Grand Tourist's sojourn in Penang was complete without a little trip outside the city: up Penang Hill and/or to the beaches at Batu Ferringhi. Today, a jaunt up Penang Hill, situated about two miles away from Georgetown in the suburb of Ayer Itam, is as atmospheric as it was in the past. While trundling up the wonderfully rickety and immaculately maintained funicular train to the summit, the views of the island and the Straits of Malacca are still spectacular.

The air is significantly cooler here, so, since colonial times, the hill was marketed as a health retreat and much-welcome reprieve from the sweltering tropical heat down below.

Particularly well known was the famous hotel establishment undersigned by the Sarkies' brothers — the Crag Hotel.

Opened in 1895 as the "Crag Hotel and Sanatorium", the hotel capitalised on Penang Hill's reputation. In style and service, the hotel was every bit as luxurious and decadent as its sister the E & O along the waterfront (see overleaf). Having shut its operations during World War II, it re-opened as an international school between the 1960s and '80s. Today, it sits abandoned and dilapidated, but in response to local opinion, plans are underfoot to redevelop and restore the building to its former glory.

Right, from left to right: Beach and shore front in Penang, early 1900s; palm-lined coast of Batu Ferringhi.
Opposite top: *Kek Lok Si or Temple of Supreme Bliss, a large Buddhist temple straddling the hillside overlooking Ayer Itam village in central Penang.*
Opposite bottom from left to right: *Penang Hill funicular (1923) in the 1930s; British colonials rest and rejuvenate on the grounds of the Crag Hotel, Penang Hill; View of the Crag Hotel, Penang Hill.*

> *Men who travel to Siam pass Penang and stop a few days on the island. They who go to Sumatra and Java know Penang. Visitors to French Indo-China call at Penang. Tourists going to Shanghai or Hong Kong stop in Penang. For years, Penang has been also the last picture of Malaya that those returning to England have been able to worship with saddened eyes. Penang has so often meant just the E. and O. and a word with Arshak Sarkies.*

— George Bilainkin, *Hail Penang!* (1932)

The Eastern & Oriental Hotel

The Eastern & Oriental Hotel, established in the year 1885 by the astute Sarkies brothers (see page 15), is the *grande dame* of Penang's hospitality scene. In its time, it played host to nobility and heads of state as well as literary and cinematic greats, such as British authors Somerset Maugham and Rudyard Kipling and American movie stars Charlie Chaplin and Douglas Fairbanks. Today, its tradition of hospitality continues unabated.

The product of a five-year restoration and refurbishment effort undertaken in the late 1990s, today's E & O is a stunning work of art. Stepping into its spotlessly white lobby and reception area, one is immediately entranced by its nostalgic atmosphere and old-world charm.

In the colonial days, the lobby was packed with people — Europeans primarily, in white starched collars and crinoline skirts, sweating profusely in the tropical weather. Come evening, guests gravitated to the grand ballroom (unfortunately removed in the process of the hotel's refurbishment) for one of the hotel's nightly dances, masked balls or legendary parties. Presided over by Arshak Sarkies, the hotel's stout, ebullient founder and general manager, they reached their apogee during the 1920s. Sarkies, with a *stengah* in one hand and the arm of a beautiful society lady in the other, was a legendary host.

Intoxicated by the tropical night air, or the fragrance of frangipani blossoms, guests twirled the night away to the strains of waltz music floating out from the ballroom. As they danced, they may have heard the evocative bellow of a maritime foghorn, suggesting the arrival of the passenger ship that plied the route to Malacca, and thereafter, Singapore.

The hotel's most enduring feature, celebrated since its opening more than a century ago, is its awe-inspiring view of the Malacca Straits along one of the longest private sea-front promenades in the region. In particular, its famous pool, set right by the sea, allows for quiet contemplation of shimmering waters and distant ships bringing cargo from afar, exactly as they have done for over two centuries.

Opposite: *The Eastern & Oriental's iconic luggage label.*

Left and above: *The hotel's cool swimming pool is built on its famous former back lawn, depicted in this 1920s postcard view of the then-newly constructed Victory Annexe.*

Top and bottom: The E & O's façade with date of establishment and back lawn today. **Opposite**: The hotel's numerous colonnades and corridors take one back to a bygone era.

Malacca (Melaka)

"Nor eastward far though fair Malacca lie,

Her groves embosom'd in the morning sky;

Though with her am'rous sons the valiant line

Of Java's isle in battle rank combine,

Though poison'd shafts their pond'rous quivers store;

Malacca's spicy groves and golden ore,

Great Albuquerque, thy dauntless toils shall crown!"

— Luís Vaz de Camões, Os Lusíadas (1572)

Historic Malacca

Malacca was the first of South East Asia's many colonies, claimed by the Portuguese explorer Afonso de Albuquerque in 1511, a staggering 500 years ago. Great Albuquerque, no more than a glorified buccaneer, had come in search of a fabled Eastern port city, purportedly a grand emporium rivalling Venice in wealth and ostentation. Having found his prize, the explorer laid waste to it, and occupied the city for the Portuguese Crown.

He was not, however, the first to claim Malacca for his own. The city had begun to rise to prominence in the 14th century under the leadership of a fugitive prince from Sumatra named Parameswara. By 1403, it was an established trading centre with sea-going vessels unloading in its deep-water river. It attracted the attention of Ming Dynasty China and, inevitably, Europe's colonial powers.

The Portuguese stayed for less than a century, after which the city had the dubious honour of being colonised not just once, but twice, by the Dutch, and finally, the British, each of whom stayed for about a century and a half. All three European powers left traces of themselves in the city's urban landscape, as did the Malays themselves, and the Chinese, Javanese and Bugis, all of whom had a strong presence at one time or another. As such, the city is quite literally suffused with history.

It is, as historians would put it, a palimpsest — a kind of blank canvas written on over and over again by successive writers, or civilisations, in this case. A layman's way to conceive of a palimpsest is to imagine a *mille-feuille* or layered cake, perhaps one of those red, blue and green *nonya kueh kueh* (Straits Chinese cakes) so popular in Malacca. Each layer of these beloved cakes has its own very distinctive colour, flavour and texture, yet all come together in a delicious whole. This is the same with the city: evident today are the multiple architectural styles, cultures and traditions that were laid down in the past.

The humble nature of the Malacca River belies its importance in Malacca's historic rise and fall as a great emporium-city. Flowing directly into the Straits of Malacca, it was deep enough to allow small sea-going vessels to sail directly into it. This strategic location of the river in relation to the sea supported ocean-going trade. This was probably a key reason Prince Parameswara decided to locate his capital here, and why Malacca's successive occupiers followed suit. In 1511, Afonso de Albuquerque's fleets conquered the city by first taking a strategic bridge across the river, thereby cutting off Malacca from the ocean, and from itself. The city and its populace finally capitulated from starvation. The Dutch used the same tactic to take the city from the Portuguese in 1641, commandeering the river and laying siege to the walled fortress. By the time the British arrived in the 1800s, the river still flowed through the heart of the city, but Malacca was no longer a centre of world trade.

The Malacca Sultanate (1411–1511)

Malacca is the historic seat of the greatest Malay Sultanate of all time, the one that started it all and from which many of the Sultans of Malaysia claim lineage today. It was founded by a fleeing Majapahit Prince, Parameswara, who, landing on the banks of the Malacca River, and resting in the shade of a *melaka* tree, saw a mouse deer driving a hunting dog into the water. Deciding that this was a good omen, he created a new kingdom on the banks of the river, named after the tree that had sheltered him. Formerly Hindu, he converted to Islam and changed his name to Iskandar Shah.

At its zenith, Malacca was a formidable empire and maritime power in the region, its fabled wealth known even as far away as Europe, where a Portuguese explorer Tomé Pires, having seen the city for himself, declared that "whoever is Lord of Malacca, has its hand on the throat of Venice".

When the Portuguese took the city in 1511, the ruling family fled, eventually establishing Sultanates in Perak and Johor. The story of Malacca, up till the exile of Sultan Mahmud Shah (Iskander Shah's great-great-great-grandson) is chronicled in the epic *Sejarah Melayu*, or *Malay Annals*. Commissoned in the 1600s by the Sultan of Johore, this historical treatise covers 600 years of Malay history and was written in classical Malay.

Top: Sheets from the Sejarah Melayu *or* Malay Annals, *dated 1896.*
Above: Traditional Malay sailing ship with sails unfurled, 1910s.
Right: Extract of a map depicting Malaya and Sumatra (the extent of the Malacca Sultanate). Woodblock print, Sebastian Münster, mid-1500s.

Top left: *The Malacca Cultural Museum is a modern reconstruction of the Malacca Sultanate Palace, on the site where the palace was purportedly located.*
Top: *Print of a Malay village, late 1800s.*
Above: *A typical Malay house on piles, with steeply pitched roof, open shutters and ornate, brightly coloured staircase tiles.*
Left: *Street murals, lining the river, depicting scenes from the Sejarah Melayu.*

Portuguese Traces (1511–1641)

Today, Malacca feels as mediaeval as it did 100 years ago when British visitors first described its winding river and Byzantine streets in turn-of-the-19th-century travelogues. These same streets are, admittedly, thronged with tourists nowadays — an outcome of the city being inscribed onto UNESCO's honour roll of World Heritage Sites. In addition, the old town's fringes are quite literally assailed by unbridled development. Nonetheless, this is a place where the past refuses to lie dormant, where history seeps palpably and inexorably through to the present.

The thing about palimpsests is that while the top-most layer is the most visible, it is rarely the layer that is of interest. In a similar way, what is most intriguing about Malacca is its Portuguese layer, which, though having been set in place before the Dutch and the British layers, refuses to fade away.

The most famous relic from Portuguese times is *La Porta de Santiago*, also known as the *A Famosa* gate. Once part of a vast wall and fortress complex that encircled the city, it stands like a silent, lonely sentinel at the foot of a small hill on which sits the other tangible relic of these first European colonisers — the ruined church of St. Paul's, once known as *Nossa Senhora da Anunciada* or "Our Lady of Grace".

It was in and from this church that Portugal's most famous mediaeval export, the priest-explorer St. Francis Xavier, preached his message of God to all of South East Asia, China and Japan. Malacca was Xavier's professed favourite city, and after he died of a fever in Southern China in 1552, his body returned to Malacca to be interred for nine months before being taken to Goa where it still rests today. The spot where he was supposedly (briefly) buried is marked out in the ruins, and sits beside a haunting quintet of ancient Portuguese gravestones, the only ones amidst dozens of Dutch and English slabs.

Other vestiges of the Portuguese are to be found along the Malacca River with the recently opened Maritime Museum and the Casa Del Rio, a luxury hotel development in pseudo-

Mediterranean style. The former is a reconstruction of the fabled Portuguese galleon, Flor de La Mar, which was wrecked in a storm off the Straits of Malacca during the year of Malacca's conquest by the Portuguese. Paving in the Portuguese style sporting a wave-like design channeling the Senado Square in Macao surrounds the reconstructed ship. Across from the Maritime Museum sits the Casa Del Rio, seemingly existing in an alternate universe where the Portuguese never left and the Dutch and the British never came.

One aspect of that fantasy is true enough though: the Portuguese never did leave Malacca. In fact, 500 years later, they — or at least their direct descendants — are still here.

To find them, one simply has to take a short taxi ride three kilometres east of the city centre, to the rather blandly named Portuguese Settlement. There, by the shimmering Straits of Malacca, one can partake of excellent seafood and curries, cooked in a Portuguese-Creole style, also known as Kristang or Eurasian, that emerged over the course of centuries through a fusion of European and Malay tastes.

On the faces of these Kristang peoples, present also in the other two Straits Settlement towns of Penang and Singapore, one may see reflected the features of their distant seafaring ancestors, surfacing like half-effaced writing from the pages of an ancient palimpsest.

Opposite left, top: Statue of St. Francis Xavier at St. Paul's Church.
Opposite left bottom: Early 1900s view of St. Paul's Church (1521) from the Pier.
Opposite right: Pier at the Portuguese Settlement, present-day Malacca.
Above left: Gateway to the fortress of Melaka. Aquatint, James Wathen, 1811.
Above: Details on Portuguese gravestones from St. Paul's Church (top and middle); La Porta de Santiago, early 1900s (bottom).

The Dutch in Malacca (1641–1824)

Above: *Detail of a V.O.C. ship on a Dutch gravestone in St. Paul's Church.*
Below left: *The Dutch Governor-General's Residence (1660s), occupied by Malacca's Governors till 1996.*
Below right: *Malacca's Dutch graveyard.*
Opposite left: *Christchurch Malacca (1753), with colourful trishaws at front.*
Opposite right, top to bottom: *The former Dutch Administration Office (1700s) is the Melaka Art Gallery today; the Melaka Museum of Islamic Art occupies a former Indies-style residence; Dutch Square in the early 1900s, before it was painted red by the British (inset).*

Just as suddenly as they had arrived, the Portuguese were gone, removed in 1641 by warships in the employ of the *Vereenigde Oost-Indische Compagnie* (V.O.C.) or Dutch East India Company. Established in 1602 by the Dutch Republic to take advantage of the spice trade in the Moluccas, the V.O.C. became the largest corporation in the world in its time, wielding significant power, including the right to deploy armies and to establish ports and colonies in its own name.

Following its conquest of the fort-city, the V.O.C. fortified the city's already formidable walls, and, for the next two centuries, proceeded to leave its mark indelibly onto the architecture of the city. Malacca's most significant landmarks were erected by

the Dutch: these include the iconic Christ Church Malacca and the *Stadthuys*, or City Hall, both of which sit alongside a string of other institutional buildings at the foot of St. Paul's Hill.

The Dutch also altered what the Portuguese had left behind. The ruins of St. Paul's Church, for example, are those of an 18th-century building erected by the Dutch over the foundations of the earlier Portuguese one. And on *La Porta de Santiago*, one can still see the coat of arms of the V.O.C. with its distinctive merchant ship. Similarly, remains of their symmetrical, solid style can be seen on some of the shophouse facades west of the river in the area known as *Kampung Belanda* or "Dutch Village".

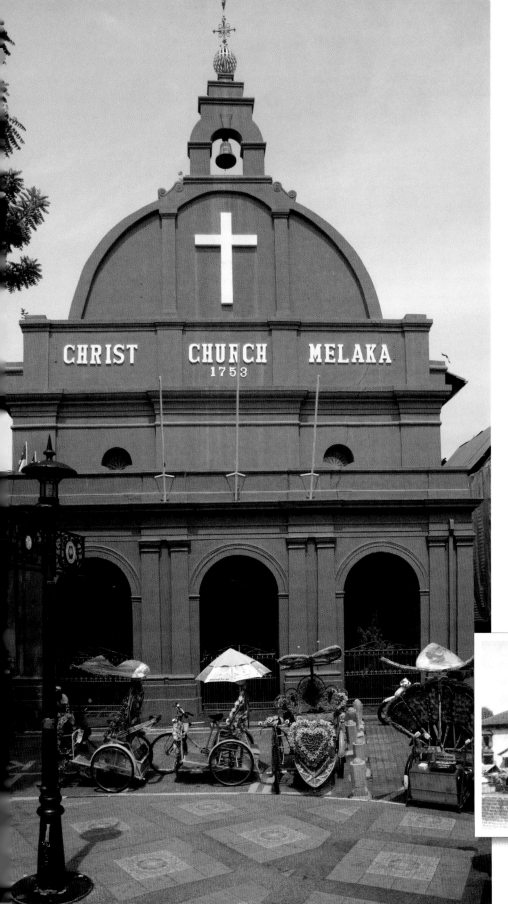

British Malacca (1795–1818 & 1825–1957)

The British came last in the game and actually ruled Malacca twice — the first colonial period lasting a mere 23 years during the Napoleonic Wars in Europe, when the Dutch briefly ceded their overseas territories to Britain. It was during this first *Interregnum* that the occupying British decided to systematically remove the ancient city walls, for which Malacca had been known for four centuries. They would have removed all traces of these had Sir Thomas Stamford Raffles not arrived in 1808 and put a stop to the destruction. In doing so, he preserved *La Porta de Santiago* as it stands today.

The British returned Malacca to the Dutch following the end of the Napoleonic Wars, but this would prove to be short-lived. As part of the Anglo-Dutch Treaty (1824), Malacca was ceded back to the British in return for Bencoolen in Sumatra. From then until 1946, it, Penang and Singapore were governed as a single colonial territory known as the Straits Settlements.

Malacca was the lesser of the three port cities. The British did not invest much by way of infrastructure or civic buildings, choosing to occupy what the Dutch had left behind. That said, look hard and you'll find numerous instances of the British period: the Queen Victoria Fountain (1901), the Moorish-style former Malacca Club (1912) and dozens of shophouses which still bear the names of old British trading companies.

Left top: The twin-spired Church of St. Francis Xavier (1856).
Left below: The Queen Victoria Fountain (1904) in Dutch Square.
Top: Bungalow in the suburbs.
Above: The Malacca Swimming Club dating from the 1930s.
Opposite, clockwise from top left: Bird's eye view of Malacca, late 1800s; Tan Beng Swee Clock Tower (1886), 1900s; the Malacca Club today (presently the Proclamation of Independence Memorial).

The Golden Chersonese

In the late 1870s, the celebrated English author and explorer, Isabella Lucy Bird, married name Bishop, (1831–1904), having completed travels through Japan and China, decided, on a whim, to make a detour south to the Malay Peninsula, and in particular, to Malacca.

She had been intrigued by stories of the "Golden Chersonese", a term used since mediaeval times and derived from the Latin *Chersonesus Aurea* or "Mountains of Gold". A certain Claudius Ptolemy, writing from Roman Alexandria in the year 150 AD, had used the term to describe the Malay Peninsula.

Arriving in Malacca, she wrote: "Malacca fascinates me more and more daily. There is, among other things, a mediaevalism about it. The noise of the modern world reaches it only in the faintest echoes; its sleep is almost dreamless, its sensations seem to come out of books read in childhood."

These words, amongst others, were later incorporated in Ms. Bird's most famous book, *The Golden Chersonese and the Way Thither* (1883), which reintroduced a whole generation of Grand Tourists to the idea of Malacca and the Malay Peninsula as an ancient civilisation of note.

Chinese Malacca (from the 1400s)

In her book, *The Golden Chersonese and the Way Thither*, Isabella Bird remarked that Malacca was "to all intents and purposes a Chinese city". That observation still holds true today. As in Penang and Singapore, the largest ethnic group in Malacca is the Chinese, occurring in the same diversity of "tribes" as in Penang.

The Chinese architectural legacy is as significant as that of the other alien occupants of the city. In addition to the numerous shophouse rows, there are some stunning complexes such as the Cheng Hoon Teng Temple, the oldest temple in Malacca built in 1645, and the Chee Family Ancestral Mansion, an imposing home built primarily as a place of worship.

Two landmarks, in particular, are unique to the city. The first is *Bukit Cina*, purportedly the largest Chinese cemetery outside of China, occupying a small hill at the edge of the Old Town. The cemetery is a public park today, affording silent, contemplative strolls amidst pleasant woodlands and thousands of traditional Chinese graves, some stunningly elaborate.

At the foot of *Bukit Cina* sits the other important landmark, the Sam Po Kong Temple. Constructed in 1795 and dedicated to the inimitable Admiral Cheng Ho, known locally as Sam Po Kong or the "Eunuch of the Three Treasures". Admiral Cheng Ho, a Muslim eunuch, was known for leading fabulous treasure fleets from Ming China all the way to the coasts of India and Africa. He visited Malacca six times, each time leaving behind men who later intermarried with Malay women, giving rise to today's Peranakan Chinese. If St. Francis Xavier is Malacca's patron saint, Admiral Cheng Ho is the city's resident deity. A small but imperious statue of him can be found within the compounds of his namesake temple, where devotees from all over Asia come to light joss sticks in his name.

Next to the temple is an ancient well, constructed in the 1450s by Chinese men in the entourage of the Ming Princess Hang Li Po. According to legend, the Princess, hand-picked by the Ming Emperor, arrived on one of Cheng Ho's treasure ships; her destiny was to marry Sultan Mansur Shah, ruler of the glorious Malacca Sultanate.

Left top: Statue of Admiral Cheng Ho in the Sam Po Kong Temple.
Left below: Two ladies dressed in their colourful sarong kebayas.
Opposite top, left to right: *Chee Family Ancestral Hall (1906), Heerenstraat; traditional Chinese shophouse; one of the many Chinese temples in Malacca.*
Opposite bottom: *Airwell of a Chinese merchant's house.*

Jonkerstraat & Heerenstraat (Young Men's Street & Gentlemen's Street)

Jonker Street and Heeren Street run parallel to each other across from Malacca's European town, and are traditionally regarded as the city's Chinatown. The twin streets were originally laid out in the Dutch era, with the latter street catering to gentlemen from the upper echelons of Dutch colonial society, and the former being the hang-out place for young men who did not belong in the same class.

The Chinese started moving into the street from the late 1700s and completely re-colonised it from around the time the British arrived. Ironically, they kept the original intents of the streets intact, with Heeren Street playing host to dozens of surreal, ornate mansions commissioned by millionaire businessmen, and Jonker Street remaining somewhat more down market, with a plethora of small Chinese provision and knick-knack shops.

Today, the streets are known as Jalan Hang Jebat and Jalan Tun Tan Cheng Lock respectively, and have kept resolutely to form. The former still caters to a younger clientele, with hip cafés and boutiques, alongside backpacker hostels and dozens of shops selling local snacks and sweets, tourist trinkets and paraphernalia. The latter has a genteel air, with slightly more upmarket restaurants serving excellent Peranakan and other local cuisine, alongside art galleries and two Museums of Peranakan Culture – the Baba Nonya Heritage Museum, a stunning recreation of an early 20th-century Peranakan mansion, and the Straits Chinese Jewellery Museum.

The Majestic Malacca

Unlike the other cities on this Grand Tour, Malacca has no grand colonial-style hotel along the lines of the E & O or the Strand. It does, however, have The Majestic Malacca, which is sufficiently unique in the history of Malacca and South East Asia to warrant a place in this canon.

The Majestic Malacca is a singular establishment because within its history and architectural form is contained the entire story of colonialism in South East Asia. It is quite literally, a Peranakan house — a house born "of the soil" in Malaya, with mixed elements of Portuguese, Dutch, British, Chinese and Malay material culture melded together into one seamless form.

The house was built in 1929 for a Chinese businessman, Leong Long Man. It remained in the hands of the family until 1955, when it was sold off and converted into a hotel. At the time, the street it sits on, Jalan Bunga Raya, was the commercial heart of Malacca, lined with hotels, cinemas and shophouses designed in the post-war Art Deco style. For a short period of time till Malaya's independence, The Majestic Malacca became a popular meeting point for British residents, celebrities and visiting dignitaries. Post-independence, the hotel dwindled in importance, before finally shutting its doors in 2000.

Thankfully in 2006, Malaysian-based company YTL Hotels acquired it and gave it a complete makeover, adding a modern, ten-storey residential wing behind the original building, which was converted into the hotel's lobby lounge, bar and restaurant. From a 24-room guesthouse, The Majestic Malacca became a 54-room 5-star hotel; and 2008 saw it re-opening in a typically grand manner.

The "Peranakan" nature of the house's architecture starts outside, with its spacious verandah — an outdoor extension of the lobby bar and lounge. This was a typical feature of Dutch East Indies-style bungalows in Malacca and Java, where wide verandahs allowed for cool evening siestas outside sweltering interiors. The Portuguese contributed the red tiled roof of the original building, also found atop many other period houses and churches in the city, and occasionally making one feel like one had stepped into the Iberian countryside. They were also responsible for the exquisite, multi-hued porcelain tiles that covered the expanse of the verandah and the lobby of the house, and were also found in the many Peranakan Chinese houses in the city.

The British contribution to the hotel was a more recent addition. Each of the hotel's 54 rooms in its high-rise wing have been styled in the form of a 19th-century gentleman's room, complete with four-poster bed, teak finishings, Art Deco tiling in the bathroom, and, best of all, an exquisite claw foot tub.

Opposite: The entrance and historic wing of The Majestic Malacca, with the tower wing just visible behind.

Above: Interior views of The Majestic Malacca – the library, reception lobby and lobby lounge, and sweet, colonial-style bar.

Singapore

"This is by far the most important station in the East, and as far as naval superiority and commercial interests are concerned, of much higher value than whole continents of territory. If no untimely fate awaits it, it promises to become the emporium and pride of the East."

— Sir Thomas Stamford Raffles, 1819

Previous page: "View of the Esplanade" by A. L. Watson. Oil on canvas, 1900s.
Above: *The Singapore waterfront and Collyer Quay today, with its towering skyline behind and Marina Bay in front.*
Left: *Collyer Quay in the 1920s.*
Opposite left: *Early 1900s bird's eye view of Empress Place, with Victoria Memorial*

Hall and Clock Tower (1905-06), Supreme Court and the Dalhousie Obelisk (1850).
Opposite right top: *"Portrait of Sir Thomas Bingley Stamford Raffles" by George Francis Joseph. Oil on Canvas. 1817.*
Opposite right bottom: *Advertisement for John Little & Company Limited department stores, 1911.*

The Grandest Emporium in the East

In the winter of 1819, Thomas Stamford Raffles, then the Lieutenant Governor of the British colony of Bencoolen, arrived on the shores of the island of Singapura, accompanied by colleagues from the British East India Company. With only a single colony in the East Indies — the island of Penang — Raffles et al were concerned that the British were losing their toehold in the region to the Dutch, who held a monopoly over trade in the Malacca and Sunda Straits.

Raffles took one look at the island and saw what nobody else before him had seen. With its strategic location at the tip of the Malay Peninsula and its deep natural harbour, this humble island had the potential to become the "grandest emporium" the Far East, nay the world, had yet known. Shrewdly exploiting a crisis of succession in the ruling Johor Sultanate, Raffles recognised the elder son of the late Sultan as its legitimate sovereign, rather than the Dutch-allied younger brother. In return, he was allowed to establish a trading settlement on the island in the name of the Company.

By 1824, two significant treaties were concluded: the first between the Dutch and British to divide the East Indies into British and Dutch spheres of influence, accomplished through the mutual exchange of British Bencoolen for Dutch Malacca; and the second between Raffles and the newly-minted Sultan Hussein Shah of Johor, to cede the entire island of Singapore to Britain. Penang, Malacca and Singapore were thereafter governed as a single territory known as the Straits Settlements; and Singapore began its inevitable rise to become the greatest colonial capital in the Far East.

The city proper was born on the humble banks of the Singapore River, where Raffles first made landfall. Through a shrewd policy of free trade wherein no import duties were levied on any ship wishing to dock and trade in the harbour, Singapore grew to prominence in a very short time. Junks from China, *perahus* from Bugis, dhows from Araby and steamships from Europe chose to dock here, bringing with them goods

John Little & Company Limited
The "Harrods" of the East

New premises in Singapore

SINGAPORE and KUALA LUMPUR

Special attention given to outport orders in connection with the Rubber Industry
General and Planters' Catalogue on application

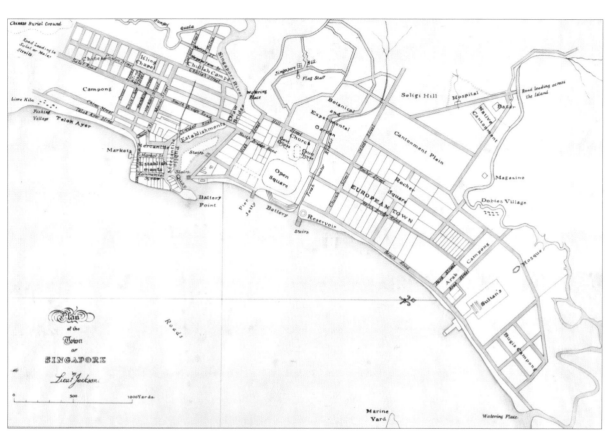

from all over the world, alongside thousands of merchants, traders, civil servants and coolies. This burgeoning multi-cultural population became the founding fathers of today's still eclectic and still entrepreneurial Singapore.

The Emporium-city wasn't a new phenomenon, of course. Singapore was the latest incarnation in an illustrious line of Emporia-cities in South East Asia, beginning with Malacca in the 14th century, then Manila and Batavia in the 15th and 16th centuries, and followed by Penang, Saigon and Rangoon in the 17th and 18th centuries. Singapore's rise, at the turn of the 19th century, signalled Penang's slow decline: once the capital of the Straits Settlements, this capital status was shifted down to Singapore in 1832.

By the beginning of the 20th century, the port of Singapore was the most important port in the Asian region, supplanting Batavia, and surpassing even new upstart Hong Kong in shipping volume and activity. Trade generated immense wealth, which in turn was invested into the city's urban landscape. Visitors recalled an Old Singapore of grand, sweeping vistas, monumental civic and cultural buildings that outshone other port cities in the British Empire, and a surfeit of elegant parks and open spaces. This still holds true today, even as Singapore continues to maintain its pre-eminent position as one of the most important ports not just in the Far East but the world; built, as it was, through the gilded sheen of colonial capital.

Colonial Capital

Today's Singapore still regards its colonial capital status with the utmost seriousness: The local authorities, taking over from where the British left off, have very shrewdly put in place an economic development approach that capitalises on Singapore's heritage, that exploits its "colonial capital" so to speak. It isn't merely that colonial-era policies of maintaining a free port and entrepôt status are still in place; it is that Singaporeans have managed to turn around everything that is — or was — colonial and use it to their economic and cultural advantage.

Let's take the Singapore River and its environs. This was once the civic, commercial and cultural heart of the colony — where people from all over the world arrived in droves to seek their fortune. Today, people still arrive in droves, with surprisingly little change in context. The banks of the river are now the centre for tourism: once humble godowns along Boat, Clarke and Robertson Quays have been restored, refurbished and renovated almost beyond recognition, transformed into a literal theme park of upscale bars, restaurants, boutiques and alien architecture. The river is also the city's financial hub, where latter-day "coolies" come to seek their fortune in the many towering bank and commercial headquarters in Raffles Place.

Heritage proponents in Singapore claim that in its rush to develop post-Independence, Singapore destroyed much of its colonial-era architecture. The neo-Palladian and Renaissance-style commercial vernacular of Raffles Place, for example, had to give way to the towering global banality of today's financial services centres. Similarly, the venerable Raffles Institution,

established by Raffles himself in 1823 on the western flank of the Padang, was demolished in the 1980s so Raffles City, the city's biggest mall at the time, could be built on that same spot.

An alternative point of view could be to consider that Singapore wasn't so much destroying its colonial heritage, as furthering the colonial vision first propounded by Raffles — that the city would be the grandest emporium the world had ever known — past, present and future. When one compares Singapore with other cities in South East Asia, the reality is that the former has managed to retain a significant amount of its colonial-era heritage even as it develops at breakneck speed. Wandering the streets of downtown Singapore, one stumbles across pockets of architecture frozen in time — areas where a palpable sense of history and Empire still remains strong.

Opposite left: Two views from Fort Canning — the gates (1846) to the Christian cemetery and the barracks (1920s).
Opposite bottom right: Government Offices (1865) at Empress Place, now the home of the Asian Civilisations Museum.
Right top: Bird's eye view of the Civic District and the skyscrapers of Boat Quay.
Right below: St. Andrew's Cathedral (1861) in the early 1900s and today.

This page: *Raffles Place in the 1930s and totally transformed today.*
Opposite bottom left: *Raffles Chambers, Raffles Place in the early 1900s.*
Opposite bottom right: *Traces of Raffles in Singapore.*
Opposite far right: *Statue of Sir Stamford Raffles at his purported landing site, Empress Place.*

Raffles — an Iconic Name

In a stroke of genius, Raffles' name itself has been transformed into a brand in Singapore. Associated with a kind of neo-Victorian luxury, it has come to represent high-end, bespoke service, a surfeit of choice and seamless efficiency, all for a price that guarantees value for money. Raffles anything has become an assurance of quality that appeals not only to Singaporeans, but to the whole of post-colonial Asia and to those once-colonial masters in Europe.

The list of Raffles-named things in Singapore is extensive and includes streets, squares, buildings, institutions, companies, and more. There's Raffles Place — home to the city's international financial centre — and Raffles Boulevard, home to the city's most luxurious hotels and malls. Of course, no visit to Singapore is complete without a visit to Raffles Hotel (see pages 86–89), the flagship property of the Raffles Hotels and Resorts Group, while across the road one finds Raffles City — today an international chain of malls in Asia. In addition, one finds Raffles Hospital, Raffles Marina, Raffles Town Club, Raffles Design Institute, Raffles Institution, Raffles Girls' School, Raffles Junior College and even Raffles Montessori (a pre-school).

The list continues to grow as the Raffles brand takes itself abroad to China, India and the Middle East; all are eager to partake in and benefit from an association with the name.

Colonial Contemporary

What distinguishes Singapore from other Asian destinations is the city-state's ability to marry the colonial with the contemporary in a seamless, sophisticated manner. Doggedly re-presenting its colonial heritage for contemporary tastes, it ensures that the former remains relevant, even highly desirable.

Singapore has one of the most progressive heritage policies in all of Asia, one that eschews objectification for something more pragmatic. Motivated by a recognition that heritage must be "living" in order to be preserved, there is support by city authorities for the development of a vibrant cultural and heritage sector nationwide, with an emphasis on making heritage and culture relevant to everyday life. Naturally, what "living" and "everyday life" mean changes with the times, so what preservation entails must similarly adapt. In fact, five

decades after independence, the colonial is still pervasive in Singapore, not just in terms of the physical architecture of the place, but also in its legal and civic institutions, its language — the official language of business is still English — and its way of life.

For glimpses of colonial contemporary, where the colonial is updated for contemporary usage and taste; or where colonial elements are appropriated or used in contemporary design; or where the colonial is juxtaposed against the contemporary; or, finally, where the contemporary itself recalls or mimics the colonial — Singapore presents a wealth of fascinating choices for the aficionado, proving that history can and must guide development in order that the latter may be true to the essence of the city.

Below left: Courtyard at the Convent of the Holy Infant Jesus (1913), converted into an F. & B. development in the 1990s.
Below middle: A colonial black and white residence (1930s), set in expansive grounds.
Below right: Government House (1869), formerly the offices and residence of the British Governor. Today, as The Istana, it is the official residence of the President of the Republic of Singapore.

Top: Interior of the Tanjong Pagar Railway Station (1931) by Swan & Maclaren.
Above: View along Andersen Bridge (1910) towards the Fullerton Hotel (formerly the General Post Office).
Right: The former Supreme Court is today's National Gallery of Singapore.

"Streets of Harmony"

While all of the colonial port cities in this Grand Tour were cosmopolitan and multi-ethnic — a direct result of colonial-era policies that favoured trade, commerce and immigration — Singapore has always prided itself on being *the* multi-cultural melting pot of the East. Besides the Europeans (which included Jews and Armenians), the population comprised three main ethnicities.

The first and the most numerous were the Chinese: hailing from a variety of south Chinese cities, like their counterparts in Penang and Malacca, they came and settled because British colonial laws, unlike those in Qing Dynasty China, allowed them to acquire private property and to accumulate personal wealth. Many of them arrived as impoverished coolies but through sheer hard work and relentless entrepreneurialism, became immensely wealthy *towkays*, or business tycoons.

The second major immigrant community was the Indians, who, like the Chinese, hailed from a variety of Indian provinces, and in particular Tamil Nadu. There were Klings from the Coromandel Coast, Sikhs from Punjab, Bengalis from Bengal, Gujarati, Sindhi, Ceylonese, Malayalees, Parsees and many others, all with their own individual rituals and traditions. They took up a range of occupations across all strata of society, ranging from merchants, moneylenders (*chettiars*), priests, policemen and coolies.

Finally, the third group was the Malays: indigenous to the East Indies and similarly diverse, they included Malays from Singapore and the Malay Peninsula, Javanese and Madurese from Java, Minangs from Sumatra, Bugis from Sulawesi, Boyanese from Bawean island, and so on. The Malays were intensely communal, living their lives entirely within their own

villages (*kampongs*) and family circles, ruled over by the Sultan of Johor, from his royal palace compound in Kampong Glam.

A unique feature of all three Straits Settlements' towns, home to almost all of the creeds and religions in the world, were streets known as "Streets of Harmony", where on the very same street were to be found significant places of worship from each of the major religions in the city. Penang has its Pitt Street, known today as Jalan Masjid Kapitan Keling and Malacca its Temple Street, known today as Jalan Tokong. Both of these were strongly promoted in the cities' bids for UNESCO World Heritage Site status, and today are popular tourist destinations.

In the case of Singapore, there are at least three that could possibly be in the running. The first is the fraternal twins — Waterloo and Queen Streets — with their Catholic churches, Hindu temple, Chinese temple and even a Jewish synagogue. The second is Telok Ayer Street, one of the oldest streets in Singapore with the most stellar historic credentials. In the 1800s to the early 1900s, this street fronted the harbour (its name means "bay water" in Malay) and it was where

Chinese and Indian immigrants first set foot on the island. As a consequence, it is home to some of the oldest temples, mosques, churches, as well as Chinese clan associations, all of which served as immediate communities for the new arrivals. The final street is South Bridge Road, just north of Telok Ayer Street, which served as a border between the Chinese and Indian neighborhoods. On one side of the street sat rows of Chinese shophouses, and on the other, a mosque and Hindu temple catering to Indians of Hindu and Muslim persuasion.

Because the most important Chinese and Indian places of worship in Singapore — the Thian Hock Keng temple on Telok Ayer Street and the Sri Mariamman Hindu temple on South Bridge Road feature here, it is appropriate to also throw in the equivalent for Singapore's Malay Muslim Community: the Sultan Mosque. Even though it sits in its own precinct, the royal compound of Kampong Glam, a bit away from the Streets of Harmony, it is a marvelous Indo-Saracenic structure designed, surprisingly, by the colonial architects of Messrs. Swan & Maclaren, and also has Turkish, Persian and Moorish influences.

Opposite: Thian Hock Keng Temple (1842) on Telok Ayer Street, in the 1920s (top) and today (inset).
Above, from left to right: The Church of St. Peter and St. Paul (1870) on Waterloo Street; interior of Thian Hock Keng Temple; Sri Mariamman Temple (1843), on South Bridge Road; Sultan Mosque (1928), Kampong Glam.

The Garden City

Besides being known as a free port, Singapore is also famous for being a "Garden City" — a verdant, luxuriant city in a garden. The origins of this Garden City heritage can be traced back to the establishment of the Singapore Botanic Gardens in 1859 by the British colonial government, who established similar botanic gardens everywhere they had a toehold — Penang, Calcutta, Hong Kong, even in Buitenzorg in Java (today's Bogor) when the island was briefly held by the British.

Nearby Orchard Road was a landscape of orchards and plantations that, even when cleared in the mid 1800s to the early 1900s, remained leafy and suburban with dozens of ornate villas housing wealthy European and later, Chinese business magnates. By the 1930s, the trees had been cleared and Orchard Road became a popular destination for shopping and entertainment — yet it still remained leafy and green, even post independence.

It was also post independence that the authorities began to experiment with the concept of the "Garden City" in a big way. Urban planners decided that even as the city urbanised, the extent of green cover should grow in tandem, in order that the city be amply shaded from the sun; and that the cityscape be pleasing and restful to the eye. They achieved this by lining major streets and highways with towering, tropical trees and shrubs, such that one had the illusion of never leaving a tropical rainforest.

The city centre, in particular, void of greenery in the late colonial era, began to resemble a vast park — a literal extension of the Botanic Gardens that sits at the city's edge. In addition, park and urban planners have recently developed a round-island network of park connectors which, in effect, transforms the entire island into a walkable, cyclable park. A new Gardens by the Bay was also inaugurated in 2010, adding 100 hectares of green space to a new downtown area that sits on reclaimed land.

In the meantime, the Singapore Botanic Gardens — the *grande dame* of gardens, so to speak, continues to play a vital role in the city-state's cultural and recreational life. It is held dear by Singaporeans and foreign residents alike, and is regarded as a national and world heritage site in Singapore.

Above: A view of the Singapore Botanic Gardens, early 1900s.
Right: The iconic bandstand in the Gardens today.
Opposite left: The "Super-Trees" in Singapore's Gardens by the Bay.
Opposite right: Edred John Henry (E. J. H.) Corner House, in the Singapore Botanic Gardens (top); portrait of "Mad" Ridley (bottom).

Henry "Mad" Ridley and the Malayan Rubber Industry

Even though the initial function of the Singapore Botanic Gardens was purely recreational, by the 1870s the gardens had become a centre for scientific research, later playing a  significant role in the establishment of rubber as a major cash crop in Malaya.

In 1888, the naturalist Sir Henry Nicholas Ridley became the first Scientific Director of the Botanic Gardens, and he embarked on a crusade to research and promote the commercial use of rubber. Just 10 years before, rubber seedlings had been smuggled out of Brazil to gardens all over the British empire — London, Calcutta, Java and Singapore.

Sir Ridley's breakthrough came in 1895, when he discovered a way to tap rubber of its latex without damaging the trees. For many months after, he tried to convince Malayan plantation owners to switch from coffee to rubber instead, earning the moniker "Mad Ridley". By the time he retired from the Gardens in 1911, his efforts had paid off — Malaya became the world's largest producer of rubber, fueled by growth in the automobile industry. Sir Ridley would become known in history as the "father" of the rubber industry.

Singapore's Grandest Hotel

Raffles Hotel is the quintessential grand hotel, the *grande dame* to rival all the other *grandes dames* of South East Asian hospitality. Its story begins in 1887, two years after its sister hotel, the Eastern & Oriental, the eldest of the brood, was established in Georgetown, Penang. Buoyed by the latter's success, Tigran Sarkies, the second of the Sarkies' Brothers, took his capital and entrepreneurial spirit down south to establish a hotel establishment worthy of the grand colonial emporium that Singapore was poised to become.

The original Raffles Hotel occupied a 200,000 square-foot seafront location along Beach Road. In the beginning, she was a mere bungalow on the beach; but the ever-enterprising Tigran would not stand still, expanding the hotel in the course of the next decade — first the Palm Court Wing in 1894, then the stunning neo-Italianate Main Building in 1899, and finally the Bras Basah Wing in 1904, just before he passed away.

In its time, Raffles Hotel has hosted a glittering cast of celebrities and writers, including Rudyard Kipling, Joseph Conrad, Herman Hesse, Ava Gardner, Elizabeth Taylor and Noel Coward, to mention a few. However, the one person most associated with the hotel is Somerset Maugham (1874–1965), who, in 1921 and 1926, stayed at Raffles while gathering research for his book *The Casuarina Tree*, a collection of short stories about colonial life in Malaya. Later, he allowed the hotel to use his name and a quote (above) in their promotional material and there is also a suite named after him. In 1959, he returned for a last time to bid his farewell.

Up until the 1970s, just after Singapore's independence, Raffles Hotel was the toast of the town. At almost any hour of the day or night, the place was quite literally bursting with activity: cruise liners dropped off hundreds of tourists, eager for a sumptuous feast in the hotel's dining room, and residents of the colony danced the night away in glamorous society balls and parties in the ballroom. Today, however, the hotel maintains a restrained and rarefied air: Access to the lobby and its residential wings is now restricted to residential guests only, with all incidental and boisterous tourist activity

Opposite: The entrance to Raffles Hotel today; Raffles Hotel luggage label, 1920s.
Left and above: The iconic façade of Raffles Hotel in the early 1900s and today.

relegated to its attached arcade, where the Long Bar, famous for being the origin of the Singapore (gin) sling, and a small theatre have also been relocated.

Today's Raffles is a product of a complete restoration that "returned" the hotel to its benchmark year of 1915. The hotel entrance, shifted to the side of the main building for much of the '70s and '80s, was returned to the centre of the main building; the rooms and suites were completely refurbished; and the grand ballroom, which once occupied the front of the building, was torn down and replaced with a simple, yet elegant, cast-iron portico. The restoration was completed in 1991, and went on to inspire a flurry of similar grand hotel refurbishments in the region, saving many of these other *grandes dames* of hospitality from demolition.

Opposite: Interior views of the Raffles Hotel, including the grand lobby and lobby bar, colonnades along guest suites, the cast-iron fountain in Palm Garden, and one of the dining establishments.

Above: One of the many garden courts in the residential wing of Raffles Hotel.

Right: Raffles Hotel ballroom in the 1920s (inset) and now.

Batavia (Jakarta)

" 'What do you think of that?' asked Rienkie's mother, pointing at the painting. 'A real Indies sky, don't you think?' And only a few people could reproduce an Indies sky, she went on to say. To do that you must have lived in the Indies for a long time. In fact, you really had to be born in the Indies."

— Robert Nieuwenhuys, *Faded Portraits* (1954)

The Netherlands East Indies

One hundred years after the Portuguese and Spanish galleons arrived in the East, and almost 200 years before British fleets did, the Dutch came in their merchant ships of the *Vereenigde Oostindische Compagnie* (V.O.C.) and established the largest contiguous colonial territory East of the Suez.

Dropping anchor in Batavia on the island of Java in 1619, the Dutch expanded their presence throughout the Malay Archipelago over the next three centuries, using a combination of shrewd realpolitik and outright (armed) force to wrest over dominions from indigenous Javanese and Malay princes. They would remain in these islands until 1946.

But before that, the Nederlands-Oost-Indië, or Netherlands East Indies, as this colonial territory was called, was the stuff of fairytales. It was a vast, endless place, extending from the island of Sumatra on the western tip of the Malay Archipelago, to the western half of the island of Papua New Guinea. At its heart was the island of Java, the jewel in the crown. Home to a 2,000-year-old indigenous culture and civilisation that had produced otherworldly monuments like the sacred Buddhist mountain of Boroboedoer, and the Hindu temples of Prambanan, it was a fertile and mystical place, evoking shimmering rice terraces as far as the eye could see, and fiery volcanoes spitting out smoke and lava.

Given the vastness of the Netherlands East Indies, the Dutch never gained a total foothold over the interiors of most of the colony's larger islands. But in Java, their rule was absolute. The Javanese kings and princes were complicit in this, ceding *de facto* rule to the colonial government in return for being recognised and propped up as symbolic and god-like "regents" of their own traditional dominions. With no need for governing, these princes instead focused their own attentions and their not insubstantial income received from the Dutch, on developing the traditional arts, allowing for a rich tradition of elaborate craft, courtly dances, literature and ritual to flourish, particularly in the twin royal capitals of Soerakarta (also known as Solo) and Djokdjakarta.

Alongside the royal capitals, the Dutch established their own string of cities on the island. In the East there were the multi-cultural port cities of Soerabaja and Semarang, the second and third largest and most important cities of the colony. To the west there was Buitenzorg (meaning "carefree"), known for its splendid Governor's Palace and legendary Botanical Gardens; and Bandoeng, with its pleasant climate and its art-deco architecture.

Finally, there was the capital of the colony, Batavia. Conjuring a grandiose vision of fabulous wealth, canals reminiscent of Amsterdam, tree-lined boulevards and monumental buildings, it was a potent symbol of Dutch colonial might and enterprise.

Previous page: Recoloured print from Meyer's Universum, 1842.
Top: The Susuhunan of Surakarta, from J. F. Sheltema's Peeps At Many Lands — Java, 1912.
Above: Wajang Wong, traditional Javanese dance based on the Hindu epic, the Ramayana.
Above right: Netherlands East Indies postcard, 1900s.
Opposite, clockwise from top: Map of the Netherlands East Indies, 1903; Mt. Merapi; Boroboedoer.

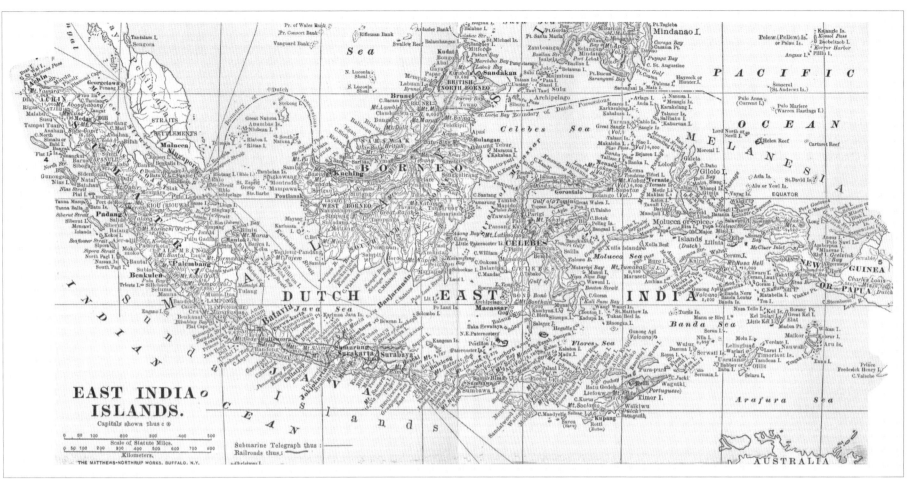

EAST INDIA ISLANDS.

Capitals shown thus ⊙

Scale of Statute Miles.
0   50 100   200   300   400   500

Kilometers.
0 50 100   200   300   400   500   600   700   800

THE MATTHEWS-NORTHRUP WORKS, BUFFALO, N.Y.

Submarine Telegraph thus ⁚
Railroads thus ⁚

Oud Batavia

Modern-day Jakarta traces its roots back to 1619, when it was established by officers of the V.O.C. as the Dutch colony's strategic base on Java. The Belanda people, as the Dutch were called in Malay, would go on to conquer the entire expanse of today's Indonesia — all 17,000 islands. The man credited with conquering and founding Batavia, Jan Pieterszoon Coen, is still here today in the city he founded, albeit three metres under the soil, in an almost-forgotten and poorly maintained grave in the recesses of the city's Wayang (Shadow Puppet) Museum, once the site of its main church.

The immediate vicinity in which the Wayang Museum and Coen's grave sits is today known as Kota (which simply means "city"). This small expanse of 1.3 square kilometres is the oldest part of Jakarta, and the very heart of Oud Batavia (Old Batavia) itself. Here, one finds the largest concentration of colonial-era civic and commercial buildings, with the most impressive of these sitting around the present-day Fatahillah Square, the former Stadsplein or City Square; and along the banks of the Kali Besar, formerly the Grootegracht, or Grand Canal.

Buildings, however, are poor windows into past ways of living; and in any case, while some effort had been made to preserve building exteriors in Kota, very little in the way of what went on inside has survived. Oud Batavia today is an empty shell — a mere façade in most cases. The world that once inhabited it, the world of the Indische, or "indigenous" Dutch peoples, has vanished without a trace.

The Indische

A mere century ago, the Netherlands East Indies was populated by a strange peoples, evolved from having been born and bred in the Indies for more than two centuries. They were outwardly European, or at least Eurasian (mixed-race), and they had their own unique culture that blended European sensibilities with Javanese superstition and aesthetics. Their speech was peppered with Malay phrases, and most of them were fluent in Malay.

One way of conceiving of the Indische is to see them as Peranakan Belanda (*peranakan* simply means "of the soil"), equivalent to the Straits Chinese communities today, with their fusion cultures and proficiency in Malay. Another, perhaps more appropriate way to conceive of them, is to regard them as the Asian equivalents of the Afrikaners in South Africa, the Dutch-speaking peoples who, like the Indische, colonised South Africa and developed their own distinctive culture and language. They too, had been in South Africa since the early 1600s, though, unlike the Indische, they are still there.

In the photo, the unique Indische culture is readily apparent: the mothers — the *njonja besars* (here I'm using the Dutch, rather than the English transliteration of Malay) — are wearing *sarong kabaia*, the formal dress of Malay and Peranakan ladies throughout the Malay and Indonesian Archipelago. Amongst the Indische, the *sarong kabaia* was a mark that one was of the soil, born and bred in Java, rather than fresh off the boat. It was a mark of distinction and class and signified old money, rather than *nouveaux riches*, or rather, *nouveaux arrivés*.

Post Indonesian independence in 1946, many of the Indische were forced to leave the Indies, where they had spent the better part of their lives, for an ancestral homeland that some of them had never seen. Many were "repatriated" to The Hague, and peering out of their tiny windows upon the wintry and utterly alien landscape of Holland, an entire generation of these exiled peoples felt an incomparable sense of loss for a past that could never return. They had a term in their mother tongue for this crushing sense of loss — *tempo doeloe* or "time past".

Opposite, top to bottom: The historic Amsterdam Gate (1600s); Port of Batavia, Kota Toea and the Great Canal today.
Opposite right: Batavia Stadhuis, by M. T. H. Perelaer, 1888 and today (inset).
Above: "Young Lady in Rocking Chair, Batavia 1869". Oil on canvas. Jan Daniël Beijnon.
Left: Dutch family in an Indische-style villa.

The Port of Batavia

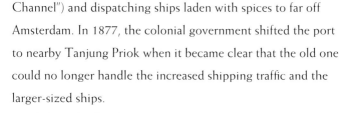

Jakarta is a port city, and the ancient Sunda Kelapa port is its place of origin. The port has been operating since the 13th century, in the time of the Sunda Kingdom, from which it gains its name. Then, as now, craft from all over the Malay Archipelago docked here in order to transport pepper and other spices to distant lands across the sea.

When the Dutch arrived in the 1600s, they took over the port and expanded it, renaming it Havenkanaal ("Port Channel") and dispatching ships laden with spices to far off Amsterdam. In 1877, the colonial government shifted the port to nearby Tanjung Priok when it became clear that the old one could no longer handle the increased shipping traffic and the larger-sized ships.

Today, the Sunda Kelapa port is still in operation, but only serves *pinisis* boats — mid-sized schooners that shuttle between Java and neighbouring regions, in particular Bugis, Makassar and Mataram. Near the port itself stands the old Harbourmaster's Tower (De Uitkyk, 1839), which is attached to the present Museum Bahari or Maritime Museum. The museum occupies 17th-century V.O.C. warehouses, built along the remaining section of wall that once encircled Batavia and was demolished by the Dutch in the 18th century.

In the shadow of the Harbourmaster's Tower stands the Vismarkt, or fish market, known today as the Pasar Ikan. Established in the 18th century, the market has been continually in operation since then. Every morning at dawn, the fisherfolk display their catch — thousands of fish of all kinds from across the shimmering seas of the Netherlands East Indies Archipelago.

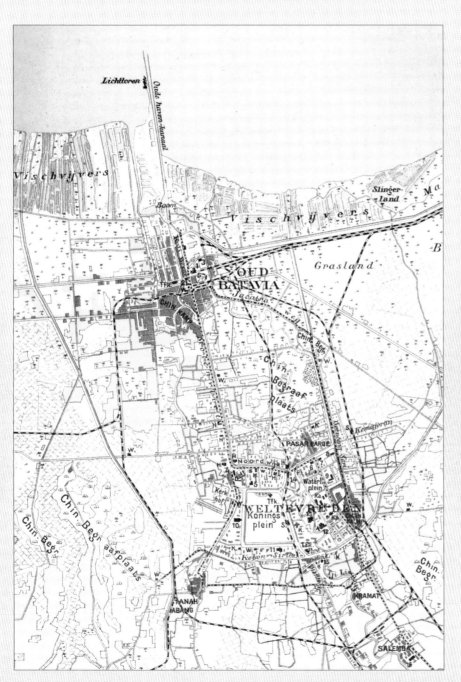

Map of Batavia

Batavia was laid out along a north-south axis that extended from the old Havenkanaal (today's Sunda Kelapa) in the north, through Kota Toea, or Oud Batavia, to Weltevreden in the South. At the southern edge of Oud Batavia stood Glodok, the city's Chinatown (marked as "Chinesche Kamp" on the map). Glodok used to look like any other Chinatown in South East Asia with its traditional Chinese shophouses and temples. But today, save for a few temples still standing, most of old Glodok has vanished.

Opposite: Pnisis boats at the Sunda Kelapa port today (top), the Harbourmaster's Tower today (inset) and by Perelaer, 1888 (bottom).
Above: Glodok, the city's Chinatown, around the 1920s.
Left: Map of Batavia, 1917.

Growth of a City

Batavia, like Jakarta today, consisted of a series of precincts along a north-south axis. At the very north was the Old Town or Kota Toea, the administrative and commercial heart of the Dutch colony. In the 17th and 18th centuries, this was Batavia: a mediaeval walled fortress of a city, like its contemporary, Malacca. Within the fortified walls of the city stood a castle overlooking the harbour, from whence the V.O.C. administrators sent forth their merchant ships to Europe.

Its main artery was the Grootegracht or Great Canal. Now known as the Kali Besar, it is along the *gracht* that one finds the greatest concentration of historic buildings in the city. The former residence of the Governor-General of the Dutch East Indies, built in 1730 and known today as the Toko Merah or Red House, and the former Stadhuis or City Hall (1710) are prime examples. Also here are some more elaborate Indo-European edifices that used to house commercial and trading establishments and a number of Dutch Indies-style residences, with large shuttered windows and

expansive verandahs to maximise ventilation. Of note are the half a dozen former bank headquarters, built in the Modernist or Art Deco styles, along Jalan Bank.

By the early 1800s, the Dutch had had enough of their walled city by the sea, with its stagnant canals infested with malaria-bearing mosquitoes. Drawing a few disparate suburbs together — suburbs with quaint names like Noordwijk (North District), Rijswijk (Rice District) and Molenvliet (Mill Stream) — they created an entirely new city centre to the south of the fortress. Called Weltevreden or "Well-contented", it became the civic, military and cultural headquarters. Flanking a new city square known

as Konigsplein, or King's Square, for much of the 1800s till the 1940s it was known for its verdant, tree-lined avenues and row upon row of beautiful residences. Postcards from the era show an idyllic and tranquil landscape straight out of the Dutch countryside.

Today, much of colonial Weltevreden is gone, and the area, now Central Jakarta, is an ugly, built-up, traffic-congested urban space — the antithesis of *weltevreden*. Where one is most likely to still get a sense of the past, however, is around Merdeka (Independence) Square, the former Konigsplein, where many Dutch-built civic institutions still stand. A visit to the National Museum of Indonesia, previously the Royal Batavian Society of Arts and Sciences, is a must. Founded in 1778, its patrons and stewards briefly included Sir Thomas Stamford Raffles during the Napoleonic Wars in Europe in the mid 1800s, when the Dutch Republic ceded control of its overseas territories, including Java to Britain. Today, the museum contains an outstanding collection of Hindu and Buddhist art from pre-Islamic Java (4th–15th centuries), aptly portraying a deep-seated Indian influence in the island's history and culture.

Opposite left, top to bottom: Menteng, early 1900s; Dutch Governor-General's Palace (1873), Perelaer, 1888; Michiels Monument (1850s), Perelaer, 1888.
Opposite right: Advertisement for the publishers, G. Kolff & Company, 1930s (left); Konigsplein, Weltevreden, 1920s (right).
Above left: Williamskerk (1834), Perelaer, 1888.
Above right, top to bottom: De Javasche Bank building; Toko Merah (1730); interior of Café Batavia.

> *The Hôtel des Indes was very comfortable, each visitor having a sitting-room and bedroom opening on a verandah, where he can take his morning coffee and afternoon tea. In the centre of the quadrangle is a building containing a number of marble baths always ready for use; and there is an excellent table d'hôte breakfast at ten, and dinner at six, for which there is a moderate charge per day.*
>
> — Alfred Russell Wallace, *The Malay Archipelago* (1869)

In Memoriam — Hotel Des Indes

HOTEL DES INDES
WELTEVREDEN (BATAVIA)
JAVA
THE PREMIER AND MOST MODERNLY CONSTRUCTED HOTEL IN THE DUTCH EAST INDIES.

Above: Advertisement for Hotel Des Indes, 1930s, noting how it was "the premier and most modernly constructed hotel in the Dutch East Indies".
Right top: *Hotel Des Indes' classic luggage label, early 1900s. Note the Dutch flag.*

The Hotel Des Indes was the oldest and most famous grand hotel of them all. Established in 1856 in Batavia, the most important trading port in the Dutch East Indies and possibly in South East Asia at the time, its reputation spread far and wide across the globe.

The hotel was situated in the affluent residential precinct of Weltevreden, alongside sumptuous villas and broad, tree-lined boulevards. In those days, visitors arriving at the port of Batavia recalled the pleasant journey by horse carriage or motorcar to the area, and the gleaming white marble façade of the hotel appearing like a mirage out of the greenery.

Even by today's standards, the Hotel Des Indes was grand. Historical brochures described the accommodation and cuisine as being "unsurpassed", and included a picture of its massive dining saloon, seating over 500 persons. The hotel was renowned for its fabulous *rijstaeffel*, immense multi-course dinners served by a bevy of liveried waiters, which saw traditional Indonesian dishes from across the Dutch East Indies accompanied by rice.

Tragically, the hotel's strong association with Dutch colonialism sealed its doom post-1949 in the patriotic climate of independent Indonesia. In 1962, an indignant President Soeharto established Hotel Indonesia as a competitor to the then already government-owned and failing Hotel Duta Indonesia (as the Hotel Des Indes had been renamed). Ten years later, unable to accept the continued presence of this insult to Indonesian independence, Soeharto finally demolished the *grande dame* and replaced it with a featureless mall.

Today, a Carrefour hypermart sits where Hotel Des Indes used to stand, and the entire Weltevreden district is no longer recognizable, having become a mess of malls, apartments and slums, like most of Jakarta.

Incidentally, after Indonesia's independence, a generation of Dutch Indische and Indo (mixed-race) families were "repatriated" en masse to the Netherlands, most specifically The Hague. Even though it was a place they had very little connection with culturally, it now gives a nod to the past with the many *rijstaeffel* restaurants in the city.

It is also home to another Hotel Des Indes, established in 1881 by the Dutch King Willem II. Its name was a nod to these returning emigrés from the Dutch East Indies and it too became the grand hotel of the city, hosting royalty, heads of state and celebrities. Fittingly enough, the cast-iron portico at the entryway to the hotel still bears the coat of arms of Batavia.

Above: Classic photograph of the Hotel Des Indes in 1931.
Right, clockwise from left: *Lobby lounge of the Hotel Des Indes; Rijstaeffel; the hotel's dining room.*

Soerabaja (Surabaya)

6

"And now all of Java was celebrating, perhaps also the whole of the Netherlands
Indies. The tricolor fluttered joyously everywhere: That one-and-only maiden of the
photograph, goddess of beauty, beloved of the gods, was now ascending the throne.
She now was my queen. I was her subject. [...] And my queen would never know that
I had walked this earth."

— Pramoedya Ananda Toer, *This Earth of Mankind* (1980)

City of Heroes

As a city, Surabaya predates the Dutch conquest, having been the seat of various independent Javanese Sultanates in the 15th and 16th centuries, before falling to the Dutch East India Company in 1743, a full century after Batavia.

It is thought that the name "Surabaya" is derived from two words — *sura* meaning "shark" and *baya* meaning "crocodile". This etymology is supported by a popular East Javanese legend, which tells of an epic offshore battle between a monstrous shark and crocodile, which, in turn, is believed to refer to the 1292 battle between a Javanese prince, Raden Wijaya, and the Mongol fleets of Kublai Khan. In this battle, which took place in east Java, the former defeated the latter and went on to found the mighty Majapahit Empire.

During the 18th century, the V.O.C. developed Surabaya into the second largest port in its time in South East Asia, after the regional headquarters of Batavia. The city went on to become the largest naval base in the region from the 1800s. As a major trading port and emporium, Surabaya established an open, multi-cultural and cosmopolitan urban landscape similar to other port cities in the region, notably Penang, Singapore and its sister city, Batavia. Besides the indigenous Javanese, the city was home to a large population of resident Chinese, south Indians and Arabs, each group housed in its own racially-segregated quarters as in Singapore. These quarters and their residents still exist today, in the city's historic Old Town.

Unlike Batavia, which was irretrievably linked to the Dutch and thus hit harder by a wave of Indonesian nationalism after the colonial era, Surabaya is, by a stroke of fate, strongly associated with the Indonesian Independence movement. It was here, in the heart of the Old Town that the Battle of Surabaya — no less than the battle for Indonesia herself — was fought in 1945. Here too, over the city's grand colonial hotel, was the red and white pennant of independent Indonesia ripped from the Dutch Tricolour like a newborn babe.

To Indonesians, Surabaya became known as "Kota Pahlawan" or the "City of Heroes" — the city of Indonesia's making. This association with nationalism, coupled with a general lack of will or resources to demolish and redevelop, and topped off with the Indonesian government's over-riding focus on Indonesian-ising Batavia, resulted in Surabaya being left largely as it was after Independence. As such, it is an atmospheric place to visit with an intact urban fabric that reveals its various layers of history.

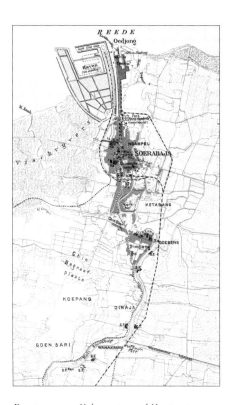

Previous page: Kalimas river and Kampong Baroe, early 1900s.
Opposite, clockwise from top: *The Red Bridge; Indische family and traveller's palm; port of Tanjong Priok; Heroes' Monument.*
Above: *Map of Soerabaja, 1917.*

Kalimas — River of Gold

The Kalimas, or "River of Gold" in Javanese, bisects Surabaya, flowing all the way from the mouth of its colonial-era harbour, Oedjoeng, to the Old Town. Along the way are dozens of V.O.C. era godowns, or warehouses, that used to store goods brought in from the far reaches of the Indies. Many of them are shuttered for good, but some are still operating.

In the old days, the Grand Tourist would have ambled along the waterside up to the ancient Kalimas port, to view the fabulous sight of dozens of moored *pnisis* boats — large wooden schooners that for centuries shuttled spices and textiles between Surabaya and the island of Madura. They would then have walked further to the Naval Officers' clubhouse or Modderlust at the very edge of Oedjoeng.

These days it is not so easy to make the journey on foot. The farthest one may go is to a strategic turn in the river, where it winds to the left and disappears behind a row of godowns. At this very point, once called Kampoeng Baroe (or the New Village), the intrepid wanderer witnesses Oud Soerabaja, the city at its very essence, reminiscent of those far-flung Dutch canal cities such as Leiden or Rotterdam.

If one makes one's way to Oedjong harbour (called Ujong today) by car, one finds it still operates today as a passenger and military harbour; and that its old Harbour Tower (formerly known as the Wilhelmina Tower) still stands. In the early 1900s, to cope with an expansion in trade and the advent of container shipping, the port proper was moved to nearby Tanjung Perak.

Top: Kampong Baroe (1920s) and today.
Right: Sampans along the Kalimas River, early 1900s.
Far right: V.O.C. warehouses, 1920s.

Old Town East

Heading south along the bank of the Kalimas, one first encounters the Arab quarter of Ampel. Here, the streets are thronged with motorcars and *becaks* (cyclos) bearing families dressed in brightly-coloured clothes out shopping, visiting neighbours or simply hanging out. The stores in Ampel are run by descendants of Yemeni Arabs that emigrated to Surabaya from the 17th century onwards. Stocking many of the same products that they have always sold — textiles, dates, wondrously fragrant Arab perfumes — the scene is very atmospheric. Down by the fish market or Pasar Pabean as it is known, one catches sight of an age-old scene: local ladies haggling over the remains of the morning's catch.

Slipping into Chinatown, just south of Ampel, one comes across a completely different scene altogether: one of neglect and dereliction. However, many of the crumbling facades of these ancient streets present an extraordinary, almost Mediterranean, surfeit of colour: deep blues, seductive mauves, lime greens, brazen pinks and yellows. As many of the city's Chinese moved out of this area decades ago when the centre of economic activity shifted further south to Tondjoengan, what remains is a ghostly landscape of two-storey shophouse buildings interspersed with an older vernacular influenced by the courtyard houses of southern China.

One highlight is the Hok An Kiong temple which sits at the corner of a street delightfully named Jalan Coklat (Chocolate Street). Translating as the Temple of Fortune and Peace and dedicated to Ma Zu or the Goddess of the Sea, it is the oldest Chinese temple in Surabaya. It was erected in 1830 and made entirely from wood by native Chinese craftsmen.

Nearby is Jalan Kembang Jepun ("Jalan Japanese Village"), the very heart of Chinatown itself, once a bustling thoroughfare but today, a quiet, crumbling side street. Its name is a reference to the days when the Japanese plied these streets as prostitutes, and contemporary graffiti found on the street celebrates this once less-than-salubrious past.

Left: Hok An Kiong Temple, 1920s.
Top: *Pasar Pabean or fish market, 1920s.*
Above: *The Arab quarter of Ampel, 1920s.*

Historic Soerabaja

Across the Red Bridge, the European Town begins in earnest. It stretches for a good eight kilometres to the suburb of Wonokromo, thereby making Surabaya a city with one of the most extensive tracts of extant colonial architecture in South East Asia. It wasn't that the locals loved their old colonial masters: the Dutch were universally loathed for having treated the Javanese as nothing more than slaves, subjecting them to centuries of cash-cropping that kept them impoverished and dependent. The fact is that Independence brought no reprieve to poverty and the entrenched class system in Javanese culture and there were neither resources, nor will, to demolish these buildings. Thus, they remained and were re-occupied by banks, government institutions and wealthy Javanese families — the successors to the colonial Dutch land-owning class.

The most impressive instances of colonial architecture occur by the banks of the Mas River along Jalan Rajawalli and Jalan Jembatan Merah, previously known as Willemstraat and Willemskade respectively. Here sit the headquarters of old trading and merchant houses — the Dutch were, after all, a nation of merchants — and there is a cleanness and no-nonsense functionality to the architecture that distinguishes it from the more ornate English, Spanish or French colonial tradition found elsewhere in South East Asia. Many of the buildings, however, have not aged well and are in dire need of restoration. A large expanse of colonial-era villas has also been cleared recently to make way for a spanking new mall.

One of the most significant landmarks in the vicinity is the former headquarters of the Naamloze Vennootschap (N.V.) Maatschappij Tot Exploitatie van het Technisch or Society for the Exploitation of Technology ("N.V." denotes a publicly-listed company), erected in 1916 with an ostentatious Moorish-style dome. An un-missable symbol of the old town along Jalan Rajawalli, it is known more familiarly to the locals as the Cigar Building. Further west sits another famous landmark — the headquarters of the Nuts-Spaarbank or Savings and Utility Bank, erected in 1914 and sporting a Dutch-style clock tower. Both buildings remain in a good state of preservation, alongside others from the era, making for street views that have remained largely unchanged for almost a century.

Left top: The Nutspaarbank Building, on Willemskade.
Left below: The Cigar Building today and in the 1930s (inset).
Opposite right, top to bottom: *Views of the old town in the early 1900s, including Willemskade, Societeitstraat and Pasar Gelap.*
Opposite far right: *The Red Bridge in the early 1900s (top), in the midst of the Battle for Surabaya (bottom right), and today (bottom left).*

The Red Bridge

The Old Town is split into the European and Asian (Chinese and Arab) quarters by the Kalimas River, over which extends the Roode Brug or Red Bridge. This bridge is significant in the history of modern Indonesia as it was here that the Battle of Surabaya — the most important pro-Independence struggle against Dutch and British re-occupying troops — was initiated in 1945. This occurred just weeks after Sukarno's declaration of Indonesian Independence in the aftermath of World War II, and the Dutch colonial regime's repudiation of this declaration.

On 26th October, as a British Brigade Commander's vehicle passed through the Red Bridge area, the vehicle was surrounded by Indonesian militia and, in the ensuing skirmish, the Brigadier was hit and killed by a stray bullet. All out war ensued, with more than 6,000 Indonesian resistance fighters losing their lives. They are commemorated by a Heroes' Monument in the city and by a public holiday, Heroes' Day, on 10th November, the day the war ended.

As for the bridge, it still stands today and is known by its Indonesian name, *Jembatan Merah*.

South of the Red Bridge lies Jalan Pahlawan (Heroes' Street), previously known as Aloon-Aloon Straat, *aloon-aloon* being Javanese for public square or *padang*. Here stand the most magnificent and better preserved pieces of civic and commercial architecture, spanning more than 100 years. These include the Gothic Surabaya Cathedral (1800s), the spectacular, twin-domed Soerabaja Handelsblad Building, and the Gouverneur's Kantor or Governor's Offices (1931).

Aloon-aloon Straat leads to Toendjoengan, today's Jalan Tunjungan area. Here, the Dutch built an entirely new city in the 1930s, transforming what was once a suburb into a new commercial centre in exuberant Art Deco style. Today one finds the occasional colonial-era bungalow amongst the more recently built high-rise malls and apartments. Squat,

compact, single-storeyed, red-tile-roofed affairs, such villas stand mutely behind shut gates. The most spectacular of the colonial-era buildings is the Raad van Justitie, or High Court Building (1795), which also functioned as the Governorshuis, or residence of the Dutch Governor of East Java. It still stands today and is used as a venue for formal state receptions.

Literature from the Dutch East Indies

The four greats of Dutch East Indies' literature are Edward Douwes Dekker (1820–1887), better known by his pen name of Multatuli, Edgar (E.) du Perron (1899–1940), Louis Couperus (1863–1923), and Robert Niewenhuys (1908–1999).

Dekker, of pure Dutch ethnicity, invented the genre with his seminal and only novel published in 1860 — *Max Havelaar, of de Koffi-veilingen der Nederlandsche Handel-Maatschappy* or *Max Havelaar, or The Coffee Auctions of the Dutch Trading Company*, in which he exposed the corruption and racism inherent in the Dutch colonial government in Java. The book incited outrage in the Netherlands and lead to fundamental changes in how the colonies were managed. Couperus, also a *totok* or pure Dutchman, is known for his masterpiece and only novel set in the Indies – *De Stille Kracht* or *The Hidden Force* (1900), in which he tells the tale of a colonial regent's family, plagued and finally destroyed by supernatural forces.

Du Perron and Niewenhuys were Indos (part Dutch, part Javanese) and born in Java. Du Perron authored the acclaimed *Het Land van Herkomst* or *Country of Origin* (1935), an autobiographical novel that compared his childhood in the Dutch East Indies with time spent in Europe. Niewenhuys authored a similarly autobiographical novel, *Vergeelde Portretten uit een Indisch Familiealbum* or *Faded Portraits* (1954), in which he tenderly and nostalgically recalled scenes from his childhood while interned in a Japanese concentration camp during World War II. Niewenhuys is also known for his *Oost-Indische Spiegel* or *Mirror of the East Indies* (1972), a comprehensive survey of Dutch East Indies' literature. He is further known for having grown up in the famous Hotel Des Indes in Batavia as his father was the hotel's general manager. He spent his formative years in the hotel's expansive grounds and rarefied atmosphere, in the midst of its fashionable and oftentimes famous guests.

Native Son

Pramoedya Ananda Toer (1925–2006) is the most significant Indonesian author and freedom fighter of the modern era. While he wasn't born in Surabaya, he got a head-start in his journalistic and writing career in the port city, and has been associated with the city ever since. He is also best known for *The Buru Quartet*, a series of four political novels set in Surabaya and Jakarta.

Written in the 1980s, in post-independence Indonesia, the world of the Quartet was that of the Dutch East Indies in its final years just before and during World War II. The lead character, Minke, is a Javanese aristocrat who, choosing a literary career, gradually grows into his role as an independence fighter. The Quartet is so-named because it was written during the time Toer was imprisoned by President Soeharto on Buru island for having purportedly been involved in Communist activities. Today, *The Buru Quartet* remains one of the most polemical and influential works of Indonesian literature. Its setting in Surabaya also cements the city's reputation as the "City of Heroes".

Hotel Oranje

Hotel Oranje (today's Hotel Majapahit) is an anomaly in grand hotel terms, because it is the only hotel that played a pivotal role in a post-colonial independence movement. It was here, on 19th September 1945, that a young Javanese resistance fighter, incensed by the raising of the Dutch flag over the hotel at the end of World War II, tore off the lower blue segment of the offending flag to create what would become the red and white pennant of the Republic of Indonesia. This singular event probably also explains why the hotel still stands, while the Hotel Des Indes in Batavia was demolished.

Named after the Dutch Royal Family, the hotel is the youngest of the grand hotels of South East Asia apparently linked to the Sarkies Brothers — "apparently" because it was built in 1910 not by the main Malayan branch of the family who established the Raffles, the E & O and the Strand, but by a secondary, Javanese branch of the family, headed by one Lucas Martin Sarkies, a son of Martin's and nephew to Tigran, Aviet and Arshak. So, it wasn't quite one with the rest, but was still related.

The hotel's style recalls that of its cousins: whitewashed colonial façades embellished with Mogul-style cupolas and colonnades, a proliferation of tropical gardens and bubbling

Opposite: The leafy courtyard in the North Wing as it looks today.
Far left and left: Hotel Oranje's Art Deco façade today and in the 1950s.
Top: Hotel Oranje's luggage label.
Above: A plaque commemorating the opening of the hotel by Lucas Martin Sarkies' baby son, Eugene Lucas Sarkies, on 1 June 1910.

fountains, and stained glass windows adorning many of the walls. Inside the hotel walls, the noisy, traffic-plagued city of Surabaya can hardly be heard or felt; and the general feeling one has is of floating along in a kind of Persian Garden: a secret, enclosed space inspiring intimate, magical scenarios.

Each of the hotel's suites is fronted by its own verandah, recalling Dutch Indies-style bungalows with their majestic front porches on which the Dutch-Indonesian families, in colonial days, were wont to be seen in the evenings taking respite from the tropical heat. The suites' interiors are scented with *melati* (jasmine) and appointed with period hardwood furniture and furnishings, affording a deliciously old-world feel.

Nostalgia buffs will find it easy to imagine their suites once accommodating a long-staying guest from elsewhere in the Netherlands East Indies — a *tuan besar* dressed in planters' uniform, sporting a thick bushy beard and smoking a long pipe of pungent tobacco. From within, a wife, or most likely, a mistress — probably Indo or mixed race — emerges with a tray bearing local sweets and a glass of gin. She is wearing a form-fitting, elaborately embroidered silk *kabaia* and brightly-printed batik *saroeng*, a garment that many mixed-race and European ladies wore as a mark that they had been born and bred in Java; and she is smiling. The scene is set for a clandestine encounter — one that bears all the hallmarks of a time long past.

Opposite, left to right: *Interior views of the Hotel Oranje, including a grand staircase, the entrance to the ballroom and colonnaded corridors.*
Above: *The original, Mogul-style entrance to the building was superseded by the Art Deco façade in the 1920s.*
Left: *This postcard shows the original entrance in the early 1900s, part of which still stands today (as seen above).*

Bangkok

"There it was, spread out largely on both banks, the Oriental capital which had yet suffered no white conqueror... ."

— Joseph Conrad, *The Shadow Line* (1917)

Previous page: *18th-century engraving of royal barges before Siam's previous capital Ayutthaya on the Chao Phraya River basin.*
Above: *Wat Benchamabophit (1911).*
Right: *The many sons of King Chulalongkorn, from a newspaper article, 1901.*
Far right: *Wat Salapoon, Ayutthaya.*

Siam and Colonialism

Bangkok, the royal capital of the Kingdom of Siam (today's Thailand), is important in the history of South East Asia because it never succumbed to any European colonial power. In other words, there is no colonial history of the city — even though it came very close to having one.

Just over a century ago, in 1893, French warships sailed up the Maenam Chao Phraya or the River of Kings intent on forcibly taking this ancient empire as the French equivalent of British India. It took some deft foreign policy and significant territorial concessions on the part of the then Siamese monarch, King Chulalongkorn, also known as Rama V, of the still ruling Chakri Dynasty, for Bangkok to avoid becoming the capital of French Indochina.

The king, himself, we know well. Most latter-day Grand Tourists remember him from when he was a little boy getting to know his very persistent governess, Anna Leonowens, in the 1956 Hollywood movie musical, *The King and I*. Educated in the western tradition, he proved to be a vanguard, modernising his kingdom and playing British insecurities against French egocentrism so shrewdly that he managed to secure from both Great Powers a promise to ensure the independence and neutrality of his Kingdom.

Having no colonial history, however, doesn't mean Siam has no relation whatsoever to colonialism. Make no mistake about it: while Thailand was never a colony, Siam was a colonising power, exerting its influence over Laos and Cambodia (which it conceded to French Indochina), and the primarily Malay Muslim region along the Kra Isthmus, of which the provinces of Kelantan, Trengganu, Perlis and Perak were conceded to British Malaya. A trip to Laos and Cambodia will reveal just how pervasive the Thai cultural influence still is in these countries.

At the same time, Siam, being independent of any colonial empire, paid host to Europeans from almost every creed and language. The Portuguese and Dutch were the first to arrive in the 1500s and stayed for more than 400 years. Then there were the French in the 1600s, the Danish in the 1700s, the British in the 1800s, and finally the Americans, with their investment dollars, after World War II. At the turn of the century, the mighty Chao Phraya River was the stage for a grand pageant of empire and diplomacy.

Top left: Postcard and cigarette player's card bearing the flag of Siam – a royal white elephant against a red background. Above: Portrait of King Chulalongkorn.

The City of Angels

Most people outside of Thailand recognize the name "Bangkok" as the country's capital city. Its actual, formal name, bestowed by King Rama I of the Chakri Dynasty in 1782, goes as follows: Krung Thep Mahanakhon Amon Rattanakosin Mahinthara Ayuthaya Mahadilok Phop Noppharat Ratchathani Burirom Udomratchaniwet Mahasathan Amon Piman Awatan Sathit Sakkathattiya Witsanukam Prasit. This translates as something to the effect of: "City of Angels, Great City of Immortals, Magnificent City of the Nine Gems, seat of the King, City of Royal Palaces, Home of Gods Incarnate, erected by Visvakarman at Indra's behest". Thais simply call their capital city Krung Thep or "City of Angels".

In the early 1800s, Krung Thep was a floating city bisected by canals (*klongs* in Thai), much like Venice and Amsterdam still are today. European visitors hailed it as the Venice of the East, gleaming with golden temples or *wats* and quaint villages built entirely over the water. The Chao Phraya River was the heart of that old city, linking it to the outside world, and bringing goods and people from all over that outside world to Siam. Visitors in the early 1900s recalled the river teeming with European ships, Chinese junks and sampans, and on very special occasions like the King's Birthday, the magnificent Royal Barge, cruising upstream in a great show of pomp and majesty.

1. *Palais à Banckock*.

Today, the river plays a less important economic and political role, as the city has outgrown its traditional boundaries to become a sprawling, skyscraping metropolis — the second largest city in South East Asia after Jakarta. However, it's still a significant cultural site, affording visitors splendid views not only of the Grand Palace, the iconic Wat Arun or Temple of the Dawn and the Old European Town, but also dozens of glittering five-star hotels and mall developments.

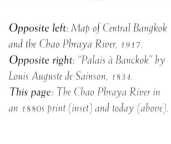

Opposite left: *Map of Central Bangkok
and the Chao Phraya River, 1917.*
Opposite right: *"Palais à Banckok" by
Louis Auguste de Sainson, 1834.*
This page: *The Chao Phraya River in
an 1880s print (inset) and today (above).*

The Europeans in Bangkok

Europeans have been in contact with Siam since the days when Ayutthaya served as the country's fabled floating capital (1500–1767 AD). The Portuguese and the Dutch had embassies in the city, and King Louis XIV, the Sun King, sent an emissary to the King of Siam in 1685, hoping to establish trade. In the 1700s Ayutthaya was destroyed by the Burmese and the capital shifted south to today's Bangkok. The Europeans followed. They were given their own *farang* (foreigner's) quarters at Bang Rak, a marshy bank along a bend of the river, as far south of the Grand Palace as the Siamese could imagine.

Here, the Europeans built their own mini-cities, with foreign legations and attached religious and civic institutions. The Portuguese established their legation in the early 1700s, and the building still stands today as the oldest foreign embassy in the city. Nearby stands the Holy Rosary Church (1786), built by descendants of Portuguese previously resident in Ayutthaya. Further south sits the French Legation, established in the mid 1800s, the second oldest and probably the most significant legation in the city. It was here that French ships docked in 1893, with their cannons aimed at the Grand Palace, poised to take the city forcefully as the jewel of French Indochina. Behind the legation stands the Gothic Assumption Cathedral (1919) and its associated Catholic Mission.

The most interesting edifice on the waterfront, however, is an Italianate building dating from 1901 which housed the Far East headquarters of the Danish East Asiatic Company or the Det Østasiatiske Kompagni (D.O.K.). Situated south of the French Legation, this shipping and trading company was founded by Hans Niels Andersen in 1897 in the Danish capital of Copenhagen. Modelled along the lines of the British East India Company and the Dutch V.O.C., it never quite established a major presence in the region, except in Bangkok. Today, the East Asiatic Company building sadly stands abandoned and deserted. However, unlike the British and Dutch East India Companies, the D.O.K. itself continues to operate under its English moniker the East Asiatic Company (E.A.C.). Another interesting fact: its founder, H. N. Andersen, also established the Oriental Hotel just next door to his offices.

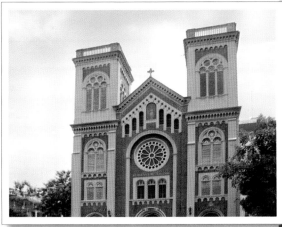

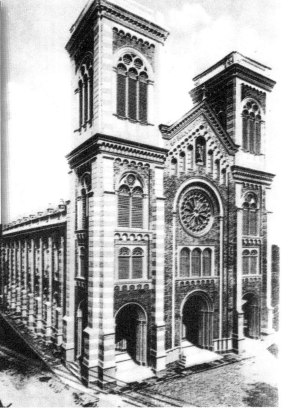

Opposite left top: The French Legation.
Opposite left bottom: The Portuguese Legation.
Opposite right: Late 19th-century photograph by Robert Lenz captures some Europeans crossing the Chao Phraya River.
Top: Hua Lamphong Station, designed by an Italian architect in 1916.
Right and above: Assumption Cathedral, Bangkok, in the early 1900s and today.
Right top: Portrait of Anna Leonowens.

The English Governess

In 1862, an English widow, Mrs Anna Leonowens (1831–1915), accepted an invitation to travel to the Kingdom of Siam as governess and tutor to the wives and the children of King Rama IV, better known as King Mongkut. The king, anxious to have his progeny learn the modern, scientific ways of the west and weary of missionary-tutors who had no qualms preaching while teaching, received and installed Mrs Leonowens at the Siamese court, where she remained for almost six years.

Her sojourn in Siam formed the basis of her two best-selling but sensationalist "autobiographies", *The English Governess at the Siamese Court* (1870) and its sequel *Romance of the Harem* (1873), both of which made her extremely famous. They, in turn, spawned another novel — Margaret Landon's *Anna and the King of Siam* (1944). This was adapted in 1956 into the immensely popular Broadway and film musical, *The King and I*, thereby immortalising Anna as the archetypical English governess.

Despite the popularity of both novel and film, the Siamese Royal Family maintains to this very day that events detailed by Mrs Leonowens in her book were grossly inaccurate and ultimately, disrespectful. All movie versions of the film continue to be banned in Thailand.

This page: *The crowning glory of the Grand Palace Complex is the Chakri Maha Prasat, built by King Chulalongkorn (Rama V) in 1882. The Central Throne Hall of this building is used in receptions of foreign ambassadors, state banquets and other ceremonial purposes. The building is unique in that it consists of Thai-style roofs atop a European-style foundation.*

The Grand Palace

While Bangkok was never colonised, it was the seat of a colonial empire that encompassed most of what we now know as Indochina, and parts of present-day Malaysia and Burma. Up until the early 20th century, the Kings of Siam ruled their Empire from within the walled compound of their Grand Palace on Rattanakosin, an island artificially created from the river by a monumental canal. While the present-day monarch, King Bhumibol or Rama IX, no longer resides in the palace complex (the Dusit Palace complex further north of the city is his home), the latter is still used today on state and ceremonial occasions, and its doors are cast wide open to devotees and visitors on every other day.

The palace was built to recall Ayutthaya, the former capital of Siam which was sacked ignominiously by the Burmese in the 1767. Ayutthaya had been described by visiting Portuguese, Dutch and French visitors as a magical floating city, built upon an island in the Chao Phraya River. It too, had been a city of canals and waterways, gleaming with magnificent *wats* and golden palaces. Many of the stones from the ruined city were painstakingly towed down river in the late 1700s to form the foundations of the Grand Palace.

The very first structures in the complex were erected by King Rama I in traditional Siamese architectural style in 1782.

Left: *The Wat Phra Kaeow, or Temple of the Emerald Buddha.*
Top: *View of the multiple temple and palace spires, in different architectural styles, within the Palace complex.*
Above: *A replica of Angkor Wat commissioned by King Rama IV when Cambodia was a vassal state of Siam.*

Still standing today, they include, amongst others, the Throne Room, where the King and his descendants were crowned. Sporting sweeping roofs and stupas, all the while ornamented with *garudas*, *nagas* (sea-serpents) and other mythical creatures from the *Ramakien*, the Siamese version of the Hindu epic the *Ramayana*, they are a sight to behold. Later on, a dizzying variety of architectural styles, including Khmer, Chinese and European, were incorporated into the design and construction of many other structures in the palace grounds, resulting in a whole that is schizophrenic but never boring. All these structures are topped by the palace itself, in essence a European building, but crowned, most symbolically, with a Siamese roof.

One of the main attractions of the complex is Wat Phra Kaew, the Temple of the Emerald Buddha. Its namesake is one of the National Treasures of Thailand, taken from Vientiane in Laos in the 17th century when the latter was a vassal state. The Buddha is revered by all Thais and indelibly linked to the ruling Chakri Dynasty. The message appears to be this: whoever guards the Buddha has divine sanction to rule.

Faith in the Buddha and the monarchy has proven to be well placed. After all, Thailand is the only nation in South East Asia today that has never been colonised. And this was all due to one of the shrewdest, most progressive and far-sighted monarchies in the world. The Grand Palace is a monument not only to its power, but to its wisdom.

Above: Interiors in the Chakri Mahaprasat Royal Palace (left) and the central throne hall of the Phra Thinang Chakri Mahaprasat (right) — unique for their display of Eastern- and Western-inspired opulence.
Left: Two general views of the Grand Palace complex, 1930s – 1950s.

The Ramakien

Siam shares its national epic, the *Ramakien*, with three other continental South East Asian nations, each of which have their own name for it: the *Reamker* in Cambodia; *Phra Lak Phra Lam* in Laos; and the *Yama Zatdaw* in Myanmar. However, the origins of the work are not South East Asian at all, but Indian.

In essence, the *Ramakien* is a localised version of the Hindu epic, the *Ramayana*; and its prevalence throughout continental South East Asia and even in Java (where a version of it continues to feature in traditional Javanese dance), belies a deep Indian influence in the region that existed long before the Chinese and Europeans arrived.

The plot of the epic doesn't stray from the Indian original, with the divine lovers, Rama and Sita falling in love and overcoming great turmoil against the context of battling demons, protective gods and a whole cast of semi-divine creatures. Unlike the Indian version, however, the South East Asian versions place a stronger emphasis on the character of Hanuman, the semi-divine King of the Monkeys. He is given a larger back story and magical romance of his own (with a mermaid princess!), even as he uses his wits and risks his life to guarantee the lovers a happy ending.

Right top: Details from the Grand Palace depicting creatures from the Ramakien, including a warrior monkey (left), a lion (top right), and a duo of garudas (bottom right).
Right: Thai Classical dancers in traditional costume, early 1900s
Far right: A modern-day performance of the Ramakien.

Above: *Vintage view of the Oriental Hotel in the late 1800s, depicting its original entrance and front lawn. The original hotel building and entrance is today's Writer's Wing.*

Right: *View of the Oriental Hotel today from the Chao Phraya River. The Tower Wing stands at centre.*

The Oriental Hotel

Bangkok is well known for the Oriental Hotel (now Mandarin Oriental, Bangkok). The hotel opened to great fanfare in 1876 and its guest list is most impressive. Boasting the likes of Joseph Conrad, Somerset Maugham, Tennessee Williams, Audrey Hepburn, Elizabeth Taylor, Henry Kissinger, the late Princess Diana and many other A-list celebrities, heads of state and members of nobility, it reads like a global Who's-Who.

Today, the waterfront property is a mish-mash of buildings and styles from different eras of the hotel's evolution, but the most interesting part is the original 19th-century hotel building.

Now renamed the Author's Wing, it stands hidden behind a dense copse of trees. Guests in the 19th century arrived here by river, docking at a pier and crossing a pleasant waterfront lawn, to join the hotel's patron and other resident Europeans gathered for gin slings and light musical entertainment of an evening.

Today, the hotel by day and the hotel at night are two completely different animals: In the day, a quaint 19th-century European atmosphere lingers, particularly in the historic Author's Lounge, where one may partake of a splendid afternoon tea in rarefied environs and in the company of other Grand Tourists and wealthy ladies who lunch. At night, the hotel takes on a different vibe, transforming itself into a slick and urbane 1930s New York-style hotel, complete with beautiful waterfront restaurants, Cuban cigar bar and resident jazz quartet. This is where the legendary Bamboo Bar comes into its own: combining fine cocktails with excellent jazz, it exudes a unique old-world ambience.

*Left: Entrance to the Author's Wing today.
Its name is a tribute to the many writers who
stayed in its comfortable suites.*
Right top: The Oriental Hotel's luggage label.
*Right below: An advertisement for the
Oriental Hotel, early 1900s.*

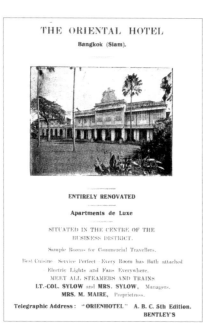

THE ORIENTAL HOTEL
Bangkok (Siam).

ENTIRELY RENOVATED

Apartments de Luxe

SITUATED IN THE CENTRE OF THE
BUSINESS DISTRICT.

Sample Rooms for Commercial Travellers.

Best Cuisine Service Perfect Every Room has Bath attached
Electric Lights and Fans Everywhere.
MEET ALL STEAMERS AND TRAINS
LT.-COL. SYLOW and MRS. SYLOW, Managers.
MRS. M. MAIRE, Proprietress.
Telegraphic Address: "ORIENHOTEL" A. B. C. 5th Edition.
BENTLEY'S

Saigon (Ho Chi Minh City)

"The steamers sailed up Saigon's river, their motors silent, taken by tugboats up to the jetties of the port along a loop of the Mékong that flanks the city of Saigon. This loop, this arm of the Mékong, is called the River, the Saigon River. The stopover was typically a week. The moment the boats pulled up against the quay, one felt like one had returned to la France. One could go out for dinner here as if one was back in la France, dance as if one was back in la France...."

— Marguerite Duras, *The Lover* (1984)

French IndoChina

Previous page: Place Garnier, with the Hotel Continental (right) and the Eden Centre (left), postcard, 1940s.
Below, left to right: Steamship at Vinh Long, Cochinchine; view of the Saigon river; the impressive Banque de L'Indochine building, on the Saigon waterfront.
Opposite left: Ha Long Bay today.
Opposite right, top to bottom: Postcard depicting the French colony of Cochinchine; Cap Saint Jacques, Tonkin; Ha Long Bay in the early 1900s; tourism brochures for French Indochina, 1930s.

Before Agent Orange, before Dien Bien Phu, and long before Ho Chi Minh, there was French Indochina or *Indochine* — exotic, evocative and emblematic of the Far East for most of the Francophone world. Today, three countries constitute the territory previously known as French Indochina: the Socialist Republic of Vietnam, the Kingdom of Cambodia and the Lao People's Democratic Republic. But what most people may not remember, is that French Indochina actually consisted of six territories, namely the Kingdom of Cambodia (a French protectorate), Laos, Tonkin, Annam, Cochinchina — the latter three territories roughly corresponding to North, Central and South Vietnam today — and a small enclave in South China called Kouang-Tchéou-Wan.

The origins of Indochina went as far back as in the 1600s, when, envious of the growth of the British and the Dutch East India Companies, the Sun King, Louis XIV, sent an emissary to Ayutthaya in 1685, ostensibly to entreat the King of Siam to open trade relations with France; but in reality, with the intent of converting Siam into a Christian, French Protectorate. That attempt to colonise Siam was foiled, as were subsequent attempts made in the 1800s, after the Siamese capital had moved to Bangkok. So the French turned to Vietnam, which, for most of the 18th and 19th centuries, saw the Nguyen Emperors undertaking a gradual incursion and annexation of territories around the Mekong Delta in the South, known as Cochinchina.

In 1859, using the expulsion of French missionaries as an excuse, French troops occupied the city of Saigon, only just unified under the Nguyen crown after a protracted civil war. In 1862, the Emperor was forced to cede all of Cochinchina and treaty ports in Annam and Tonkin to Napoleon III. In the meantime, further up the Mekong River, threatened by Siam and Vietnam on both flanks, the Cambodian King Norodom I signed his own Kingdom over as a French Protectorate, in return for France securing its independence from both Siam and Vietnam.

By 1887, the French had secured all of Tonkin and Annam. *L'Indochine Française* was born that year through the federation of the Vietnamese provinces and Cambodia, with Laos being annexed as war spoils following the Franco-Siamese War in 1893, and the territory of Kouang-Tchéou-Wan in 1898 through a lease agreement with China (on similar terms as Hong Kong to the British). *L'Indochine Française* as an entity would last till 1954, with the independence of its constituent nations. Kouang-Tchéou-Wan had earlier been returned to China in 1946 and is known today as the city of Zhanjiang.

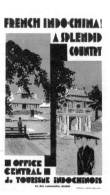

The Paris of the East

Unlike Hanoi in the north, which retains significant tracts of its Sino-Vietnamese built heritage, Saigon is essentially a French city. Between 1887 and 1902 it was the capital not only of Cochinchina, but of the whole of *Indochine*, following which the capital was moved to Hanoi.

As soon as they arrived, the French wasted no time in making the city the Paris of the East, completely destroying almost everything that stood, and replacing it with some of the most impressive, most French, imperial monuments East of Suez, particularly in and around what they nostalgically called Paris Square and down three major thoroughfares — Boulevard Bonnard, Boulevard Charner and Rue Catinat. As with their contemporaries, the British and the Dutch, the intent of French colonialism was trade, commerce and access to raw materials. Unlike them, however, the French also had one other important goal: the export of *La Civilisation Française*.

This penchant of the French to "civilise" is evident in the urban landscape of their showpiece city, Saigon. The rationally laid-out grid system with its wide, tree-lined boulevards, elegant parks, squares and roundabouts echoed the imperial city of Paris itself. So too did Saigon's monumental buildings in ostentatious Beaux-Arts, Neo-Italianate, Neo-Gothic, Art Nouveau and later, Art Deco styles.

Today, much of this still remains, clinging to the waterfront city that the French etched forcibly over the Vietnamese citadel and town that they destroyed. On the religious and cultural front, the two most famous buildings are the High Gothic Cathédrale de Notre Dame (1880) in Paris Square and the Beaux-Arts Municipal Opera House (1897) on Rue Catinat. There are also civic institutions like the bright pink Neo-Classical wedding-cake confection that is the Hôtel des Postes (Central Post Office Building, 1891), designed and built by Gustave Eiffel of Tower fame, no less, as well as the similarly eye-catching Hôtel de Ville (City Hall, 1908). Government and military installations included the *ancien* Palais du Gouvernement (Government Palace, 1873, destroyed in 1962) and Caserne de l'Infanterie (Infantry Barracks, also 1873).

In addition, within and surrounding this downtown core, sat dozens of colonial villas and bungalows housing French civil servants, merchants and their entourages — the French loved their *pieds-à-terre*. Sadly, many have been demolished in the post *doi-moi* re-building fervour of modern-day Vietnam, but a few still cling on, even as whole blocks around them are demolished for the construction of such towering hulks of nondescript-ness as the Bitexco Towers, the tallest building in the city, and the Vincom Towers, the city's most luxurious mall.

Opposite: *Cathédral de Notre Dame in the
early 1900s (top) and today (inset).*
Top: *The Palace of the Governor-General
was built in a Beaux-Arts style in 1873
but replaced in 1966 with a severe
Modernist building (inset).*
Left and above: *The Saigon Opera House
in the early 1900s and today (inset).*

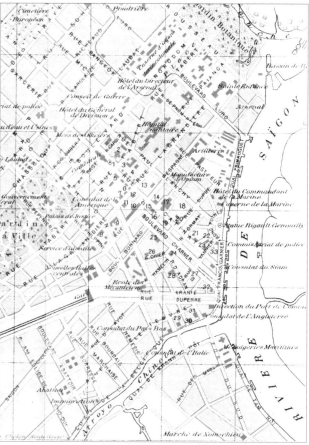

Above: *The Saigon City Hall in the early 1900s and today (inset)*.
Right top: *Locals communing in one of the many streetside cafes in today's Ho Chi Minh City*.
Right below: *Map of Saigon, 1917*.
Opposite clockwise from top right: *View of the Cholon waterfront, early 1900s; Thien Hau Temple, today; cyclos in Cholon, 1950s*.

In fact, Saigon today is a battleground of sorts — a landscape of construction and re-development. New buildings, sporting the airbrushed visages of Hollywood actresses and the serpentine logos of luxury brands, sit side by side with the earlier French legacy. It wasn't so long ago that symbols of Frenchness and Americanism were vilified as being unforgivably capitalistic and anti-revolutionary. Today, those selfsame symbols have once again become desirable marks of status and wealth.

A closer look also reveals the country's European past continuing to linger in the habits of the newly affluent Vietnamese. As they smoke, converse and imbibe *petites tasses de cafés et de thés* in the cosy cafés that line many of the city's sidewalks, they almost seem to recall the *joie de vivre et de conversation* of their former rulers. Similarly, the sight and smell of newly-baked *banh mi* or baguettes, stuffed with a variety of hams, meats, cheeses and salads; the delectable *confit de canard*, *boeuf bourguignon* or even *escargots* that can be had in the

excellent French restaurants resuscitated in the city, are a reminder that the city's French past refuses to go away. Finally, in the *boîtes de nuits* that have sprouted again in the city's fashionable corners, one can once more *aller danser comme en France* — dance like one was back in France.

Twin City

Saigon is actually a twin city or two cities in one. The French colonial settlement — Saigon itself — is set by the banks of the Saigon River and features broad straight boulevards, while the predominantly Chinese settlement of Cholon, further up the river is less orderly. The latter was established in the late 1700s by resident Chinese taking refuge from vengeful local warlords bent on massacring them for supporting the Nguyen Emperors — who were closer to the Chinese culturally — in their conquest of the South. From 1931 to 1956, Saigon was actually known formally as Saigon-Cholon, but the suffix was dropped as the former city gradually expanded and enveloped the latter.

Today, Cholon is worth a visit for its bustle and activity, particularly in and around Bình Tây market, where one may sample all manner of Chinese foods and witness all manner of exotic produce from bags of pungent black tea to dried seahorses and deer antlers, used in traditional Chinese medicine. The area is also known for its quaint and ornate temples, in particular the Quan Âm Temple, erected in the 19th century and dedicated to the Goddess of Mercy, and the Thiên Hậu Temple, erected in the same period, and dedicated to Mazu, the Goddess of the Sea. As with other South East Asian port cities with sizeable Chinese communities, one also finds row upon row of traditional shophouses adorned with colourful ornamentation and intricate Chinese characters, demonstrating again just how Saigon, and many of the port cities of the region, were joined in a network of Chinese trade and kinship that existed parallel to the European colonial one.

The French in Saigon

Notwithstanding its being known as the Paris of the East, Saigon felt more like a semi-large provincial town in the Midi or southern France — a Toulouse, say, or a Nice. At the turn of the century, before the rumblings of the Indochinese War, it was a pleasant, postcard-perfect place, eager to catch up with the times in the home cities, particularly Marseille, from whence the *paquebots* of the Messageries Maritimes, the largest and most important French shipping company in the late 1800s and early 1900s, would regularly and without fail bring the latest people, news and fashions.

Indeed, the *grand boulevards* downtown, particularly along Rue Catinat, displayed the latest hats and frocks from Paris and Marseille; and anyone who walked down these streets would also remark how the ladies here were dressed almost exactly as they were back home in France. Everything that could be had in Paris and Marseille was also available here, in the many retail shops and restaurants that dotted *le centreville*.

Where the British colonial had his exclusive Gentlemen's Club where men sipped gin slings and talked business, the French had their Cercle Sportif or sporting club — which was communal, family-oriented and focused on unbridled fun and activity. And while the British entertained themselves in private, the French did the same out in the open, on the many *al fresco* terraces and cafés along the sides of the streets. On these same streets, in the early evenings, many a Frenchman, bearded, barrel-chested and boisterous, could be seen drinking the same sweet liquors found back in the home countries, while flirting and chuckling with a bevy of pretty local ladies, French or otherwise, gathered up in his arms.

The venue for such gatherings was, more often than not, Rue Catinat. It was the most famous and fashionable street in Saigon, equivalent to the Champs-Elysées in Paris, or Orchard Road in Singapore. On this street were to be found the city's foremost fashion boutiques, supermarkets and grocery stores, cafés, all manner of retail, and also the city's most luxurious hotels and residential apartments. Named after Nicolas Catinat, a *maréchal* (marshall) of France between the 17th and 18th centuries, it was *the* place to see and be seen.

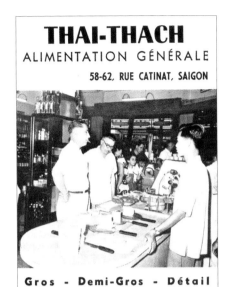

THAI-THACH
ALIMENTATION GÉNÉRALE
58-62, RUE CATINAT, SAIGON

Gros - Demi-Gros - Détail

In the course of the late 20th century, the street underwent two name changes in response to the shifting times. Between 1955 and 1975, in the thick of the Vietnam War, it was known as Tu Do or Freedom Street. Subsequently, once North Vietnam "reunified" with the South, its name was changed once again to the present, bombastic Đong Khoi or Total Uprising Street.

Today, the street has lost much of its glamour and elegance, but it is still the premiere street in Ho Chi Minh City for top hotels, luxury goods, antiques and art galleries, much like it was in the past. Quite miraculously, some of its famous establishments — in particular, all of its grand hotels, chiefly the Continental Hotel, the Majestic Hotel, the Saigon Palace Hotel and the Caravelle Hotel — continue to exist, albeit in restored and revised forms. They sit alongside spanking new mall and hotel towers that have increasingly become the visual norm on the street, threatening to overwhelm the quaint colonial atmosphere that clings on.

Opposite left: Photographs of French military officers (top) and French women and children at a Cercle Sportif (bottom).
Opposite right: Advertisement for the Grands Magasins Charner, once Saigon's foremost department store, 1930s.
This page, from top left: Advertisement for Thai-Thach, Saigon's most popular grocery store, 1950s; colonial building; Hotel Continental, viewed through the windows of the famous Givral Café (demolished); close-up of the General Post Office.
Below: Portrait of Marguerite Duras.

L'Amant

Of all the French authors of the modern era, the one most associated with French Indo-china is Marguerite Duras (1914–1996), who, in 1984, at the ripe old age of 74, published her best-selling novel, *L'Amant* or *The Lover*. A semi-autobiographical work, the story recounts a passionate but illicit love affair between a 15-year old French teenager ("the Young Girl"), freshly arrived in Saigon, and a 27-year old Chinese man ("the Chinaman from Cholon") who is heir to an immense fortune.

The book was awarded the French Prix Goncourt the year it was published and was subsequently made into a movie in 1992, directed by Jean-Jacques Annaud.

Duras herself was born in Saigon and repatriated to France at the age of 17, just after she purportedly experienced the love affair recounted in her book. Even though she was a prolific author, playwright, essayist and even film director, *The Lover* remains her most memorable work.

> *In the middle of the hotel was a small garden. Nothing was so far from the clamour of the choking, fume-ridden streets outside — the lights, the bars, the rock music, the women — that the harmony and the warm stillness of this secret garden. I sometimes went there for a late evening drink amid the frangipani and hibiscus blossom, the fairy lights and the consoling singing of cicadas. It was the reverse of the frenzy of war, and a good place to think.*
>
> — Jon Swain, *River of Time* (1996)

Hotel Continental

There are worse ways to spend an afternoon than to sit on the outdoor terrace of the Hotel Continental, sip tea and watch the world go by. Originally called the Continental Palace and built by French colonials in 1880, the hotel is situated on the celebrated Rue Catinat. The oldest and most legendary hotel in Saigon, it is the third oldest grand hotel on this Grand Tour, after the Hotel Des Indes in Batavia (today's Jakarta) and the Oriental Hotel in Bangkok.

As depicted in the movie, *Indochine*, the Continental featured prominently at the centre of the European social circle for most of the early 1900s up till the war. Catherine Deneuve's lead character appears frequently on the hotel's *terrasse*, enjoying tea or champagne with its Armenian proprietor, in the company of expatriate military men, ladies of leisure, and the occasional wealthy Vietnamese magnate.

During the Vietnam War, the hotel and the intersection it occupied were the centre of political intrigue, accommodating heads of state, spies, journalists and writers. In the 1950s, the British writer, Graham Greene passed through, staying in a suite that overlooked this intersection. He set entire scenes of his novel, *The Quiet American*, on Rue Catinat. Somerset Maugham, too, had been in Saigon three decades earlier and set one single scene in his Grand Tour travelogue, *The Gentleman in the Parlour: A Record of a Journey from Rangoon to Haiphong*, on the Hotel Continental's *terrasse*. In this scene, he described how agreeable it was to sit having an innocent drink before reading about heated affairs in the local papers. Even then, it seemed, Saigon was brewing with resentment, far from a Far Eastern idyll.

Today, the Hotel Continental is a government-managed establishment. Sadly, while it still maintains its beautiful and evocative façade, it can no longer lay claim to European luxury, nor its former status as the heart of Saigon's social scene. That has fallen to some of the many newer five-star hotels that have sprung up in the city. But, for a nostalgic ambiance, a spot of tea on its *terrasse* overlooking Rue Catinat, or a quiet drink in its courtyard garden, it still wins hands down.

Opposite left: *Peaceful courtyard of the Hotel Continental today.*
Opposite right: *Advertisement for the Hotel Continental, 1930s.*
This page: *The Hotel Continental in the early 1900s (above) and today (right).*

This page: *Hotel Majestic Saigon in the 1950s (right) and today (above).*
Opposite top: *Hotel Majestic's luggage label.*
Opposite bottom: *Arrival at the Hotel Majestic is a pleasant experience, with bellboys attending to guests' every need.*

Hotel Majestic Saigon

The Hotel Majestic opened its doors in 1925 and is a good 45 years younger than its more illustrious cousin, the Hotel Continental, down the street. It was originally built and owned by a local Chinese real-estate mogul, Mr Hui Boon Hoa, who, desirous of establishing a hotel to rival the French designed and built Continental, out-frenched the French with a palatial Art Nouveau architectural style that wouldn't have looked out of place in Cannes or Nice on the French Riviera.

Like the Continental, the hotel features in Graham Greene's *The Quiet American*. Based on Greene's experiences as a war correspondent for *The Times* and *Le Figaro* in French Indochina from 1951 to 1954, it was published in 1955. The hotel is mentioned in passing as a place for doing business in and as a sanctuary from the tedious and terrifying reality of war-torn Saigon. This is in stark contrast to the viper's nest that was the Continental, where one went to be in the thick of it all. In particular, the Majestic's rooftop bar — cooled by the breeze from the Saigon river and famed amongst wartime expatriates for its 7pm cocktails — is referred to as a slice of Paradise more than once by the main protagonist, Fowler, whenever he is caught in some horrifying circumstance in the outskirts of Saigon.

The best part of the hotel are the balconies of the river-side rooms overlooking the Saigon River and the very busy thoroughfare of Tôn Đức Thắng. Standing out here, it is hard not to imagine oneself a journalist from Paris, on assignment for the very first time *en Indochine française*. As one smoked one's cigarette on the balcony, a lover would emerge from between the sheets and approaching from behind, slip firm arms around one's waist. In the near distance, writer and lover would watch the barges, floating lethargically east to west across the river, docking inevitably at the Old Customs House by the Port of Saigon, where they would unload their age-old cargo — tea, sandalwood, lacquer, rice and other exotic produce of the East.

Phnom Penh

"It's been only a few years since King Norodom entrusted his country to France, and already all we have built in Phnom Penh has an air of agedness beneath the burning sun; the pretty and straight streets we have laid down, and which are devoid of people, are overgrown with grass; one could almost believe this to be one of our older colonies, the charm of which is made from desuetude and silence…"

— Pierre Loti, *An Angkor Pilgrim* (1912)

Kingdom on the Mekong

The history of Phnom Penh as a capital city commences in recent antiquity, when, in the sunset years of the Khmer Empire (the early 1400s), King Ponhea Yat of the Khmers briefly abandoned his splendid temple-city of Angkor and shifted his capital south to a marshy port settlement at the confluence of the Mekong and Tonle Sap Rivers. Just why the king chose to move his capital is unclear, but it probably had something to do with Angkor's ancient and sophisticated, but failing, water management systems. In any case, within 70 years, just after the king died, his successors returned the capital to Angkor briefly, then to a few other sites, neglecting Phnom Penh for three centuries.

The name of the city originates in myth, wherein an old woman by the name of Daun Penh (literally "Madam Penh"), noticing a huge *koki* tree in the waters of the Tonle Sap during its annual flood, pulled it ashore only to find it cradled multiple statues of the Buddha. Taking this as divine revelation, she rallied fellow countrymen round to construct a hillock, or *phnom*, on which a temple was erected to hold the precious relics. In commemoration of the founding of Wat Phnom ("Hill Temple"), the city was thereafter renamed Phnom Penh, or the Hill of Lady Penh.

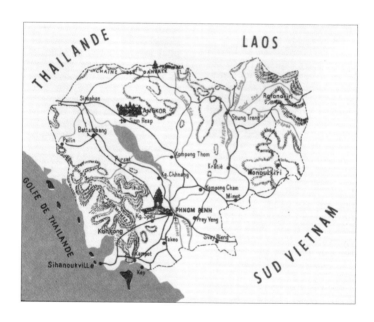

Modern-day Phnom Penh is equally imbued with a dreamlike (or nightmareish) quality depending on how you look at it. The French arrived with their gunboats and diplomacy in 1865, having coerced King Norodom I, descended from the Khmers, into signing away his Kingdom to become a French "Protectorate". They also convinced His Royal Majesty to move his capital from the marshy settlement of Oudong back to Phnom Penh.

French colonials then erected a beautiful jewel of a city here: amidst French civic buildings was built a splendid royal palace compound, modeled upon the Grand Palace in Bangkok, and complete with royal elephants, *Ramakien* murals and a Royal Ballet. All were commissioned by the King from (largely) French architects, artisans and artists.

The official status of "Protectorate" was in actuality a misnomer, as Cambodia was in all respects a colony of *la France*. Nevertheless, the Cambodian royal family, robbed of political power, invested in culture and in their own symbolic capital, becoming veritable God-kings to their people, like their descendants had been in mighty Angkor.

With the departure of the French, the Kingdom and its capital city, Phnom Penh, experienced a "golden era" in the 1950s and 1960s under the rule of the mercurial and charismatic King Norodom Sihanouk. Sadly, it did not last, and the country is probably best known internationally for its brief, bloodthirsty rule by the horrific Khmer Rouge in the late 1970s. In 1975, the Khmer Rouge, also known as the Communist Party of Kampuchea, took power in Phnom Penh, and, over the next three years, systematically murdered a full two million Cambodians, or one quarter of the population, in one of the largest political purges in history. It totally ravaged the country, which is only now beginning to recover from the scars.

Previous page: Royal elephants saddled for a walk, 1900s.
Opposite left, top to bottom: A woman of the Cambodian king's harem, 1870; seated monk, early 1900s; Cambodian boy standing before the Pont des Nagas, early 1900s.
Opposite right: Map of Cambodia from a 1950s travel brochure.
Above: A view of the five towers of Angkor Wat today.
Right top: French dignitaries, with the French colonial Governor-General of Cambodia (middle right).
Right below: Royal elephants and retinue crossing the Pont des Nagas.

Confluence of Rivers

Top right: *A view of the Mekong River flowing through Phnom Penh today.*
Below: *The Tonle Sap River in 1906.*
Bottom: *Postcard depicting the French colony of Cambodia, and the confluence of its two major rivers.*
Opposite: *Views of Wat Phnom in the early 1900s and today.*

Phnom Penh sits to the south of the Kingdom of Cambodia, at the confluence of two major river systems — the Mekong and the Tonle Sap. In Khmer times, the city was known as Chaktomuk meaning "City of Four Faces", referring to the "X" the two rivers made at their confluence, and possibly also to some notion of the city being "all-facing", or exposed to the world, like the all-facing stone effigies of Vishnu found in the temples of Angkor. From ancient times, the city was a port settlement, occupied by a Chinese majority who transported spices, lacquer, resins and other products from the Cambodian interior to the other cities of the Mekong delta and beyond.

Phnom Penh's fortunes rose again during French colonial rule, when the city served as a stopover between Saigon and the Laotian cities of Vientiane and Luang Prabang. The port area, or Quai du Commerce, was a bustling concentration of French trading companies and shipping lines, not dissimilar to Boat Quay in Singapore. Today, just like Boat Quay, the port has been refurbished and transformed into a waterfront bar, restaurant and lifestyle destination, now known as Sisowath Quay.

From Phnom Penh, the settlement of Siem Reap is a leisurely three day journey up the Tonle Sap River. In the past, and again today, the Grand Tourist travelled by boat upriver, arriving there to explore the expansive ruins of Angkor, the great temple city of the ancient Khmers (see pages 154–155).

Wat Phnom

At the very heart of the city, and the origin of the city's name itself, is Wat Phnom, meaning "Temple Hill". The *wat* was erected in 1373, though it has been successively rebuilt until the early 1900s. The complex's main stupa purportedly still holds the remains of King Ponhea Yat and his family; King Ponhea Yat moved his capital from Angkor to Phnom Penh in 1434.

Wat Phnom is ground zero in the city, a point from which all of the city's streets take reference. West of the *wat* runs Avenue Daun Penh, the heart of the French colonial quarter. South of it extends Norodom Boulevard, the city's main thoroughfare.

Colonial Quarters

Phnom Penh has one of the most charming and extensive tracts of French-style architecture this side of Paris. The colonial administrative quarter is concentrated to the north of the city centre, along Avenue Daun Penh (today's 92 and 94 Street) and surrounding Wat Phnom. Here, flanking both sides of a canal (today filled in and turned into a public park), the French built their major civic monuments, including the General Post Office (1890), the Bibliothèque Nationale du Cambodge (1924), the Municipal Police Station (1892), the Cercle Sportif (the French equivalent of the British Cricket Club, 1929), and the marvelously over-the-top Pont des Nagas (Naga Bridge, 1910s). The latter leads from Wat Phnom down to the administrative quarter, spanning the old canal and joining with Norodom Boulevard.

Along Norodom Boulevard, a major north-south thoroughfare linking the administrative centre to the Royal Palace complex, the French built dozens of magnificent colonial residential villas. Many of these still stand today. Sequestered behind high walls and lush vegetation, they house government offices and foreign embassies.

In the vicinity of the palace sits yet another cluster of French civic and cultural institutions, the highlight of which is the magnificent National Museum, built by the architect Georges Grolier in 1918 in an exuberant Khmer style. The museum houses an impressive collection of Khmer artefacts from Angkor, and is a very worthwhile preface to any Grand Tourist wishing to visit Angkor itself.

Finally, to the northwest of the city, in the middle of the Old Town with its 1930s and 1960s-style shophouses and apartments lies the surreal and iconic Phsar Thmei, or Central Market. Built in 1937 in an Art Deco style, it appears like a spaceship over the bustling streetscape, and is a fitting climax to half a century of French architectural input in the city.

This page, clockwise from top left:
The Phsar Thmei in the 1950s; the
Residence of the Governor-General with
French military band; Phnom Penh
streetscape in the 1950s; another view of
the Residence of the Governor-General.

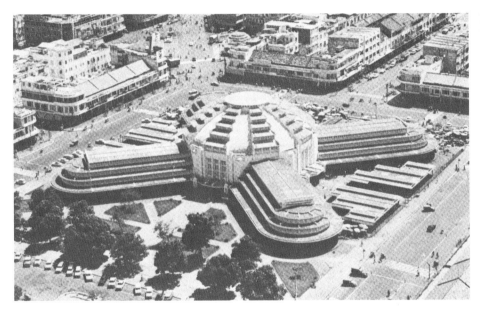

The Royal Palace

The Royal Palace complex was first commissioned by King Norodom I in 1865 when the capital was moved from Oudong to Phnom Penh. While designed by a Khmer, the palace was built by the French colonial authorities. Each successive monarch made additions to the complex, with the most recent being commissioned by King Sihanouk in the 1950s.

Modeled after the Grand Palace in Bangkok, the complex comprises the same basic structures — in particular, the Throne Hall, still used today for royal rituals and ceremonies, and the Silver Pagoda, or Wat Phra Keo, housing Cambodia's own version of the Emerald Buddha in Bangkok. Most notably, the pagoda got its name because the floors of the interior are indeed lined with plates of pure silver.

Like the Grand Palace in Bangkok, the walls of the cloisters are adorned with murals that tell the tale of the *Reamker*, the Cambodian version of the *Ramayana*. Painted in 1895, these murals are stunning works of art replete with shimmering palaces, epic battles, divine beings, and fabulous beasts. Unfortunately, they have seen better days in their more than 100 years of

existence; entire tracts are in dire need of restoration and some have even been partially erased.

Another historically and architecturally interesting structure in the complex has no Asian influence whatsoever. This is the Napoleon III Pavilion, an ornate, filigreed European-style structure sitting just to the side of the palace's administrative offices. Constructed for the Empress Eugénie of France, it was exhibited in 1869 at the first World's Fair that commemorated the opening of the Suez Canal. In 1876, not knowing what to do with the structure, Napoleon III, remarking that the "N" on its façade could stand for Napoleon as easily as Norodom, presented the structure to the latter, and it has stood in the palace grounds ever since.

Finally, no visit to the complex is complete without a quick viewing of the royal elephant stables. Up until the early 1900s, the King made regular royal processions into the city, complete with a retinue of harnessed and saddled elephants, in particular to worship at Wat Phnom. Today, however, elephants have disappeared from the palace and from the city altogether.

Opposite top: *The Royal Ballet Corps.*
Opposite below: *The ornate, filigreed Napoleon III Pavilion.*
Left and above: *The Silver Pagoda today and in the 1930s.*
Below left: *Portrait of his Majesty, King Sisowath in a 1906 Parisian newspaper.*
Below right: *Front-page coverage of the visit of King Sisowath to Paris, Le Petit Journal, 1906.*

The Cambodian Royal Family

The relationship between the Cambodian Royal Family and the French colonial authorities ran deep. Even though the French essentially ruled the country post 1865, they installed King Norodom I in the ancient city of Phnom Penh as a type of symbolic figurehead ruler.

In 1906, a remarkable event took place in French colonial history: that of the voyage of King Sisowath I — Norodom's successor — to Paris, in conjunction with the Colonial Exposition of the same year in Marseille. The Parisians were entirely won over by *sa Majesté* who exaggerated his own fairy-tale like persona by never leaving the hotel in anything less than Royal Cambodian regalia. They were also enchanted by the King's Royal Ballet company, a professional troupe of elfin young girls in elaborate and otherworldly costumes, whose performance so startled the painter and sculptor Auguste Rodin that he would use them as the subject for some of his most famous drawings.

This flair for the dramatic culminated in King Norodom Sihanouk, the great-grandson of Sisowath, who ruled Cambodia in the '50s and '60s during its golden era, and again in the '70s and the '80s in the aftermath of the Khmer Rouge period. The flamboyant, charismatic and multi-talented Sihanouk was, like his predecessor, an accomplished statesman, and also a composer, poet, author and movie director. In an inadvertent tribute to Sisowath's Royal Ballet, his son, the present King Sihamoni, is trained in the classical art of Khmer Dance.

The Ancient City of Angkor

Phnom Penh is usually taken in as a stop-over en route to the ancient city of Angkor, capital of the Khmer Empire. The city was built by the northern banks of the Tonle Sap Lake in 802 AD by the Khmer King Jayavarman II, who, fancying himself semi-divine, commissioned a brand new city to be built, complete with a sophisticated irrigation and flood management system. The highlight of the city was Angkor Wat — a massive temple and the largest religious structure in the world dedicated to the Hindu god Vishnu.

The city was inhabited for 500 years between the 9th to the 14th centuries. It was abandoned in the mid-1300s, and for another 500 years, lay deserted with the exception of bands of Buddhist monks who reverently tended to its monumental icons. Eventually, the city was swallowed up by tropical jungle, only to be "rediscovered" by French explorers in the late 1800s. Today, the entire expanse of Angkor is designated a UNESCO World Heritage Site and is one of the most visited historic sites on the planet.

This page: *An aerial view of Angkor Wat, the world's largest architectural monument. Surrounded by a broad moat, it covers 200 hectares (1.5 km by 1.3 km) and is a microcosm of the Hindu universe. The inset shows it in the 1920s, and the map is from a 1930s travel brochure.*

Opposite: *Angkor is one of the most important archaeological sites in South East Asia. Stretching over some 400 square kilometres, including forested area, Angkor Archaeological Park contains the magnificent remains of the different capitals of the Khmer Empire, from the 9th to the 15th century.*

Hôtel Le Royal

Situated in the heart of the city's colonial quarter, Hôtel Le Royal has barely changed in its almost hundred-year existence. Opened in 1929 by the French colonial authorities alongside sister hotels in Siem Reap and Hué, it very quickly established itself on the Grand Tour circuit. Phnom Penh was a convenient stopover en route to the ruins of Angkor and, while staying in the city, the Hôtel Le Royal was the establishment of repute.

Designed by Ernest Hébrard, also Phnom Penh's urban planner, and constructed between 1923 and 1924, it reflects an original and self-consciously French colonial architectural style. The embellished European façade, sloping tile roofs, shuttered windows and large, airy corridors adapted for the tropical climate are francophile through and through. The hotel's link to royalty was firm from its very inception: King Sisowath Monivong (Sisowath I's son) graced the hotel's opening reception, while his grandson, Prince Sihanouk was a frequent patron. Political, Hollywood and literary royalty also patronised the hotel when they passed through the city: the likes of Jackie Kennedy and Charlie Chaplin, and the usual suspects, Somerset Maugham, the French author André Malraux and so on, all stayed within its guest rooms and suites.

That the hotel remains standing is a miracle, given the tumultuous recent history of Phnom Penh. Between 1975 and 1979, when the Khmer Rouge seized power, the city was literally emptied of all its inhabitants, many forced into exile to the countryside, probably an equal number executed and buried. During that time, Hôtel Le Royal served as a headquarters to Pol Pot's military cadres, also doubling up as an underground food and storage facility. In the meantime, other grand colonial edifices in the city, particularly religious ones such as the city's cathedral, were demolished completely by conscript labour, using simple tools such as hammers and pick-axes.

Today, the hotel is managed by the Raffles Hotel and Resorts Group, after an extensive restoration completed in 1997. It has regained much of its old world charm, with spacious, high-ceilinged guest rooms, bathrooms with colonial-style claw-foot tubs and impeccable service, while modern trappings like an award-winning spa, upgraded business facilities and rehabilitated swimming pools further the visitor experience. One of highlights of any stay is the Happy Hour at the venerable Elephant Bar: sitting on a wicker chair beneath a lazily circulating fan with a cocktail *du jour* in hand brings up many an image from the past.

Opposite top: Hôtel Le Royal's luggage label.
Opposite bottom: The hotel logo today.
This page: The entrance and façade of Hôtel le Royal in the late 1920s (inset) and today.

André Malraux (1901–1976)

In 1923, at the tender age of 22, André Malraux, then a budding author, headed into the Cambodian jungles with two friends, in a crazy bid to loot the temples of Angkor, spirit the booty to Europe, and sell it. The French colonial authorities caught wind of this scheme, arrested and imprisoned Malraux, then put him on trial in Phnom Penh. Disgusted at the hypocrisy of the authorities, as the French government regularly helped themselves to huge chunks of the Angkor temples, he became a staunch supporter of Indochinese independence. Malraux also wrote an account in 1930 of his experience in Phnom Penh and Angkor in his seminal book, *La Voie Royale (The Royal Way)*. When out of prison, he was a regular guest at Hôtel Le Royal, and later on, he became the Culture Minister of France from 1958 to 1969.

Above left: Brightly tiled, airy colonnade outside today's Café Monivong.
Above right: The hotel lobby in the 1920s.
Left: Portrait of André Malraux.
Opposite: Hôtel Le Royal's swimming pool in the 1960s (inset) and today.

Hanoi

天報月密問來往
水色山光相送迎

"Heaven reveals the Moon's secrets, even as it waxes and wanes;
Scenes of Lake and Mountain flit by, one after another."

— Couplet, Inscription at Ngoc Son (Jade Mountain) Temple

Dragon Ascending

Previous page: Hoan Kiem Lake, early 1900s.
This page, clockwise from top: *The Kinh Luoc (viceroy of Tonkin), Gillot, 1890; pagoda of Kinh Luoc, Gillot, 1890; calligraphy at Ngoc Son Temple reads "the wind and the moon".*
Opposite left: *Hanoi Citadel Flag Tower.*
Opposite right: *Map of Hoan Kiem District, 1917.*

Of all the cities on the Grand Tour, Hanoi is by far the oldest. Founded in 1010 by the first Vietnamese Emperor Lý Thái Tô, it celebrated its 1,000th anniversary in 2010. While there are far older cities in China and Japan, that continuous, unbroken self-consciousness of being one and the same city for more than a millennium is unique in Asia. Many of its landmarks, particularly the evocatively named Hô Hoàn Kiêm, or Lake of the Restored Sword, are as old as the city itself, and still exist today even as the landscape around them has been transformed into a forest of towering condominiums and malls.

The city has had multiple names. It was first known as Thăng Long ("Dragon Ascending") and designated the Imperial Capital of the Vietnamese Kingdom. In the 1500s, it became known as Đông Kinh or "Eastern Capital" — from which the Europeans derived their term "Tonkin" when they first arrived in northern Vietnam. Finally, in 1802, it became known as Hà Nôi meaning "Between the Rivers", when the ruling Nguyên Dynasty unified the whole of Vietnam and moved the Imperial capital south to Huê.

It should be evident from this brief history that there is a deeper cultural influence at play in this city between the rivers. The Grand Tourists, arriving ostensibly to explore traces of French colonialism, discovered that a far older colonial power in the form of the Chinese had left a more enduring mark on the city and its people's cultural memory. They found out that the Chinese had colonised Vietnam for a staggering 1,000 years from the time of the Han Dynasty (100 BC) to the end of the Tang Dynasty (900 AD). Compared to that, the 80 years of French rule, during which Hanoi took Saigon's place as the capital of French Indochina, was a mere blip.

Chinese cultural influence runs so deep as to be almost indistinguishable from Vietnamese culture itself. Thiêng việt sounds like one of the southern Chinese dialects spoken,

even today, in China's southern maritime provinces. And, until the French arrived in the 18th century, Vietnamese was written using traditional Chinese script, with some variation to account for local, indigenous words.

Chinese influence also extends to the city's urban landscape and architecture. All around the Old Town are dozens of delightfully quaint, ancient Taoist and Confucian temples, built in the Chinese traditional style, still welcoming worshippers 1,000 years after the Chinese left. Here also are hundreds of Chinese shophouses. Adorning the doors, walls, front gates, lintels and arches of these temples and shophouses are a proliferation of Chinese auspicious or protective symbols — dragons and bats for good fortune; peaches or mountains for longevity; a pair of lions or door gods to ward off evil spirits. Also carved into stone across the front of these buildings, are Chinese characters: announcing the names of these buildings or couplets of poetry, many are now intelligible to only a scattering of older Vietnamese who maintain the ability to read traditional Chinese script.

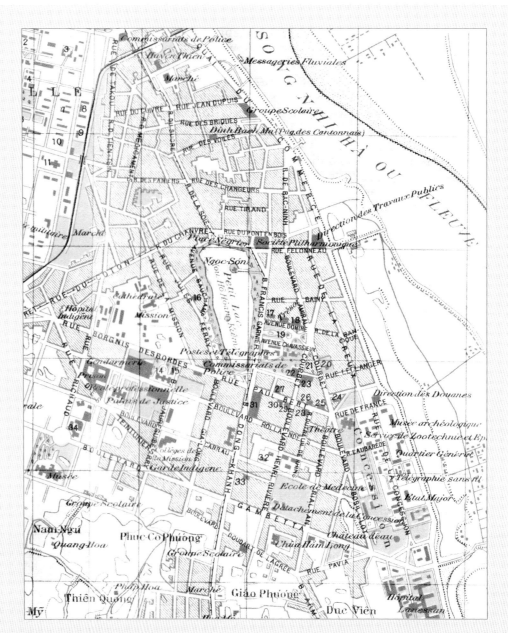

Map of the Hoan Kiem Disrict

Hanoi is centered around Hoan Kiem Lake, close to the shores of the Red River (Hóng Hà in Vietnamese and *Fleuve Rouge* in French). To the immediate north of the lake is huddled the Old Town with its 36 Streets with their 36 traditional trades. The French colonial city is built to the west, east and south of the lake, while the Quai du Commerce, or Port of Hanoi is to the north east.

Lake of the Restored Sword

Being so old means that Hanoi's origins are invariably steeped in myth and mysticism. In particular, one of the city's most enduring legends revolves around Hoan Kiem Lake and the giant turtles that inhabit its murky depths.

Legend has it that in the early 14th century when Vietnam was briefly re-occupied by Ming Dynasty China, one Lê Lợi, the son of a humble village leader, was visited by the Dragon King of the Eastern Seas. The deity bestowed upon Lê a magical sword that he would later wield to banish the Ming occupiers and restore Vietnamese sovereignty. Some time later, after Lê had founded his own ruling dynasty, the Emperor was boating on Hanoi's lake when a giant turtle rose from the depths, took the sword from the royal belt and slipped back beneath the waters. Sword and turtle were never to be found again, so the emperor acknowledged that the turtle — which he referred to as Kim Qui or the Golden Turtle — must have been an avatar of the Dragon King, come to reclaim his treasure. In commemoration of the sword's restoration, Emperor Lê renamed the lake Hô Hoàn Kiêm or Lake of the Restored Sword.

The lake is the cultural and symbolic heart of Hanoi, the centre of its civic and public life. When the Nguyen Emperors unified Vietnam and took the city from their predecessors, they built two of the city's most recognisable monuments here

— the Turtle Tower (Tháp Rùa) and the Ngọc Sơn or Jade Mountain Temple, both of which occupy their own small islets in the water and replaced pre-existing temples.

Opposite left top: *Cartoon of locals by Hoan Kiem Lake.*
Opposite left bottom: *Locals by the lake today.*
Opposite right top: *Views of Ngoc Son Temple by Gillot, 1890.*
Opposite right bottom: *1930s postcard of the same, clogged with lotus plants.*
Above: *The striking red Huc ("Morning Sunlight") Bridge today and by S. M. Salge, 1914 (inset).*
Below: *Hoan Kiem Lake and the Turtle Tower in a 1920s postcard and today (inset).*

When the French arrived, they did the same, erecting an entire new city of European-style civic, commercial and religious buildings around the lake's perimeter. Demolishing everything of cultural value to the Vietnamese, such as the old Imperial citadel of Thăng Long and the Imperial Temple Complex, they built in their place icons of French dominance.

Deliberately downplaying its significance, the French renamed the lake Le Petit Lac, in reference to the larger West Lake to the west of the city. But that name would never stick, particularly as, 600 years after the emperor "restored" his sword, giant freshwater turtles continued to inhabit the murky waters, and even today, occasionally cause a stir in the populace when they are seen surfacing to take a breath of air. Revered as guardians of the city, their very presence foretold the failure of the French colonial project.

The Old Town

The Old Town of Hanoi is an alluring creature, steeped in history, tradition and myth. Like the golden turtle of Hoan Kiem Lake, occasionally it raises its silent head from beneath the never-ending flow of traffic and people to charm the unsuspecting visitor.

In addition to the 36 Streets or the Old Quarter (see opposite), there are pockets of antiquity further west of the city, surrounded but never overwhelmed by the colonial edifices erected by the French. There is the Hanoi Flag Tower, what remains of the vast Imperial Citadel of Thăng Long, built by the very first Vietnamese Emperors in 1010 and wantonly destroyed by the French in the late 1800s. Nearby sits One

Pillar Pagoda, also erected in the early 1000s by one of the Lý emperors in gratitude for the birth of a son and heir. The French destroyed the temple in 1954, but it has been meticulously rebuilt to its original design. Finally, there is also the spectacular Văn Miêu or Temple of Literature — a Confucian temple built in 1070 to celebrate the Confucian virtues of diligence, moral rectitude and filial piety (see overleaf).

Left: One Pillar Pagoda today (top) and by
S. M. Salge, 1914 (below).
Below left: The Gate to the Old Town, one of
the few ancient structures still standing today.
Below right: The Hanoi Imperial Citadel in
the 1870s, before it was demolished.

The 36 Streets

The 36 Streets are the heart of the Old Quarter, a labyrinthine warren of streets — some hardly more than alleyways — far older than the city itself. Established by Chinese colonialists in the Tang Dynasty when Vietnam was called Annam (meaning "Peace in the South"), the Quarter used to sit just beyond the Citadel walls, which have since been demolished. When Vietnam rid itself of the Chinese, the area developed into a centre for professional guilds, specialising in a range of trades and handicrafts.

In the Chinese language, the word for "guild" or "trade" is the exact same word and character as that for "small street". As a result, rather naturally, the various guilds and trades were organised into their own streets, each named after their own particular craft.

Today, the streets still exist, but few of them specialise in their former trades. Rather, a more contemporary, mixed-use commercial landscape prevails. Hàng Bông, or Cotton Street and Hàng Gai, or Hemp Street have eschewed fabric for a host of modern fashion boutiques, tailors, art galleries, furniture and design stores, mobile phone shops, curio shops and small eating places. Similarly, Hàng Đường, or Sugar Street, no longer deals specifically with sugar but presents a mix of hardware and general provision stores, alongside the ubiquitous trinket and souvenir shops and informal eateries.

At the other end of the spectrum, two of the most delightful streets still specialising in their traditional crafts are Hàng Mã, or Votive Offering Street, which during Tết (the Chinese Lunar New Year) or Christmas, comes alive with a psychedelic array of festival-appropriate festive decorations; and Hàng Bè, or Bamboo Street, which today still presents row upon row of freshly cut bamboo, to be used in everything from construction to furniture to making traditional food receptacles.

This page, clockwise from top left:
Interior of a residence in the Old Town;
the Gate to the Old Town today; Hàng
Mã or Votive Offering Street at Tết; Hat
Street (Rue des Chapeaux), Gillot, 1890.

Temple of Literature

A prime example of how deep Chinese influence runs in Vietnamese culture is illustrated by the existence in Hanoi of a Confucian temple known as a Temple of Literature. Such temples take pride of place in major Chinese cities and other East Asian nations within China's traditional sphere of influence — Japan, Korea and Vietnam. Typically dedicated to the Chinese philosopher, Confucius, who articulated a system of thought that still underpins the politics and social structure of East Asian nations today, such temples are also schools.

The Văn Miếu or Temple of Literature in Hanoi, established in 1070 by the Emperor Lý Nhân Tông, housed both a temple and the Imperial Academy, a school for future mandarins. Those who passed the examinations had their names carved on giant stone steles borne on the backs of massive stone turtles. These still stand here today, with the oldest stele hailing from 1442 and the youngest from 1779. Many of the thousands of names carved in traditional Chinese characters on these steles are still clearly visible, and are haunting witnesses to a past long gone.

Planned according to strict principles of *feng shui*, the temple complex is laid out along a north-south axis. The visitor passes through the triple-arched Main Gate in the north, which still bears an inscription exhorting him to dismount from his horse.

Once through, he enters the first of five internal courtyards, surrounded by brick walls and presenting an oasis of calm and greenery. Past the second courtyard, the visitor comes upon the iconic Khuê Văn Các, an ancient belltower erected in 1805, and named after Kui Xing — the Chinese Deity of Literature, who also happens to be the personification of the first constellation in the Western Heavens. The stone turtles and accompanying steles appear in the third courtyard, following which, comes the temple proper — the Great Hall of Ceremonies and altars to Confucius and his disciples in the fourth courtyard. Finally, the fifth and last courtyard, destroyed by the French in the Indochinese War in 1946 but rebuilt in 2000, houses the Imperial Academy and its accompanying classrooms and dormitories. For more than 700 years, this was where the best and brightest of Vietnamese society came to be educated. Today, it stands silent and forelorn, mute testament to a millennia of living heritage that no longer exists.

Left top: Khuê Văn Các or the Constellation of Literature Pavilion, S. M. Salge, 1914.
Left bottom: A contemporary view of the pavilion known as the House of Ceremonies in the fourth courtyard.

Left and left bottom: *Two views of the various altars to Confucius and other Chinese philosophers.*
Below: *Names of scholars carved upon stone steles.*
Below middle: *The Khuê Văn Các belltower today.*
Bottom: *The main gate to the Temple of Literature in the early 1900s (inset) and today (left).*

The French Quarter

Hanoi was captured by the French in 1873, and relinquished to Ho Chi Minh in 1954. Compared to the 1,000 years of Chinese rule, the 80 years of French colonial rule seem like a mere afterthought. However, having shifted the capital of French Indochina from Saigon to Hanoi in 1887, the French proceeded on a large scale re-design of the ancient Sino-Vietnamese city. Sadly, this re-making of the city was a systematic act of cultural desecration. The city's major architectural landmarks — the Imperial Citadel and the Hanoi Temple and Pagoda Complex — were destroyed and replaced by completely incongruous and, even today, out-of-place European structures. In addition, the indigenous writing system based on Chinese traditional characters was forcefully replaced by a Latinised script.

French Hanoi was concentrated to the south, west and east of Hoan Kiem Lake and it featured many major monuments that still stand today, including the Hanoi Opera House (1911) which sits at the very end of the city's foremost commercial street, Rue Paul Bert (the equivalent of Rue Catinat in Saigon); the Société Philharmonique or Concert Hall, encroaching onto the Old Quarter in the north; the Palace of the Governor-General (1906); and a dozen municipal and bank headquarters, all of which were designed in the exuberant Neo-Classical and Beaux-Arts styles then popular in Paris. One particular edifice, the Maison Central (1898), Hanoi's prison complex, later became notorious during the war when it was referred to as the "Hanoi Hilton" and used as a prison for American POWs.

Beyond civic and cultural monuments, the French were also responsible for a proliferation of beautiful villas that dot the colonial quarter and are now home to the city's foreign embassies and missions. The same goes for the glorious Hôtel Métropole, which today continues to draw visitors from all over the world (see overleaf).

Left, top to bottom: Place Chavassieux with Hôtel Métropole to the left; Rue Paul Bert with the Hanoi Opera House at the end of the street; Boulevard Dong-Khanh with Maison Godard department store to the left. **Opposite left:** *The imposing façade of the Hanoi Opera House today.*

Opposite right, top to bottom: The Palace of the Résident Supérieur of Tonkin (1911); Maison Centrale; the Palace of the French Governor-General of Indochine (1906); St Joseph's Cathedral in the early 1900s and today (inset).

Hôtel Métropole

The *grande dame* of Hanoi's hospitality scene opened its doors in 1901 as the Grand Hôtel Métropole Palace. It was the brainchild of Messrs André Ducamp and Gustave-Emile Dumoutier, the former a wealthy world traveller and the latter an ethnographer and archaeologist working for the colonial government. Dumoutier had stayed at the Galle Face Hotel in Colombo — the first of its kind East of Suez — and, while in Singapore, had been inspired by the Messrs Arshak and Tigran Sarkies, who were overseeing the construction of Raffles Hotel at the time.

The two gentlemen predicted that with Hanoi replacing Saigon as the capital of French Indochina, there would be an urgent need for a first-class hotel establishment worthy of the city's new status and capable of receiving the hundreds of expected tourists. By the 1920s, le Métropole, had become the foremost European-style Grand Hotel in the colony, trumping the Hotel Continental in Saigon and establishing a firm reputation in most of the port cities of South East Asia as the centre of social life in Indochina.

The hotel, both then and today, is a welcome oasis from the thoroughly congested and noisy streets of Hanoi. Like the Hotel Continental in Saigon, the history of the Métropole is inextricably linked to that of the Vietnam War, with many of its headlining guests — Graham Greene, Jane Fonda, Joan Baez — having visited in that era. In addition, the hotel can boast of having hosted Somerset Maugham — he passed through here and wrote parts of his travelogue, *The Gentleman in the Parlour*, in one of the hotel's guest suites. Unfortunately, having disliked Hanoi so much — Maugham found the city enervating — he scarcely gave it a mention in *The Gentleman*.

Winter is the best time to stay at the hotel. Hanoi, a mere 1 degree in latitude south of Hong Kong, is the only other city on this Grand Tour that can boast of having an actual winter season. Wrapped up in a seasonal quilt and supping at one's aperitif in the famous Bamboo Bar inside the hotel's central courtyard, one feels transported to 1920s Paris. The hotel is lit up with a thousand christmas lights, and the lilting melody of French *chansons* waft through the air.

Another memorable experience is to take advantage of a spin through the city in one of the hotel's 1950s vintage Citroen cars. Sailing through the streets in this vehicle, with hundreds of ordinary Hanoi-ans peering curiously at one from their motorcycles, it is hard not to feel like a turn-of-the-century colonialist, ostentatiously descending onto the town for a sumptuous dinner and subsequent merry-making at the cabaret. *Que la vie est belle!*

Page 172, left: *Interior views of Hôtel Métropole.*

Page 172, right: *The Hôtel Métropole logo.*

Page 173: *View of Hôtel Métropole in the early 1900s (inset) and today.*

Above: *The famous La Terrasse al fresco café.*

Left: *Vietnamese cyclos, available for guest sightseeing excursions.*

Opposite left: *Advertisement for the hotel — and others in Tonkin, 1930s.*

Opposite right: *One of Hôtel Métropole's vintage 1950s Citroens.*

SOCIÉTÉ FONCIÈRE DU TONKIN ET DE L'ANNAM
Société Anonyme au Capital de 10.288.700 francs
Siège Social : 15, Boulevard Henri Rivière, Hanoi
— R. C. Hanoi 36 —

BRANCHE HOTELIÈRE

HOTEL MÉTROPOLE
15, Boulevard Henri Rivière
Tel : 60 et 334   **HANOI**   Ad. télég. : Métropole-Hanoi

HOTEL DE LA CASCADE D'ARGENT
au TAM-DAO (Province VINH-YÊN) Tel. : 5 Tam-Dao

GRAND HOTEL DE CHAPA (Province LAO-KAY)
Tel. : 5 à Chapa

Station d'altitude (1.550 ") dans la haute région du Tonkin, face au Fan-Si-Pan, le plus haut sommet de l'Indochine (3.142 "). | Mountain spot (4.650 feet above sea level) in the highland of Tong-King, facing Fan-Si-Pan, the highest summit of Indochina (10.300 feet).

GRAND HOTEL DU LAC à YUNNANFOU (Chine)

— WAGONS-RESTAURANTS —
Réseau Nord des Chemins de fer de l'Indochine
Northern Indochina Railways — Hanoi Vinh et vice versa

Manila

"*The city proper of Manila, inhabited by Spaniards, Creoles, the Filipinos directly connected with them, and Chinese, lies, surrounded by walls and wide ditches, on the left or southern bank of the Pasig, looking towards the sea. It is a hot, dried-up place, full of monasteries, convents, barracks and government buildings. Safety, not appearance, was the object of its builders. It reminds the beholder of a Spanish provincial town, and is, next to Goa, the oldest city in the Indies.*"

— Fedor Jagor, *Travels in the Philippines* (1875)

The Spanish East Indies

Before the Spanish arrived in the 16th century, the Philippines was just another cluster of islands at the north-eastern end of the vast island chain known as the Malay Archipelago. Geographically, ethnographically and culturally, it was very little differentiated from Malaya and present-day Indonesia: its people were essentially Malays and spoke a variant of Malay; its islands had also been welcoming traders from India, the Arab World and particularly China, for centuries; and much of the island cluster, including the Manila region, was ruled first by Hindu Kingdoms and subsequently by Islamic Sultanates.

The arrival of the Spanish changed all that. Manila was founded in 1571 AD, when the Spanish conquistador Miguel López de Legazpi dropped anchor in the vicinity and claimed everything around in the name of the Spanish Crown. Before then, Legazpi had claimed Cebu and Luzon islands, but he felt there was something stirringly different about Manila Bay. Arguably the world's most perfect natural harbour with a strategic location relative to China, Japan, the Moluccas and the Spanish Colony of New Spain (today's Mexico), he saw its potential.

When Manila was declared the capital of the Spanish East Indies, it was bestowed its own coat of arms, and was formally called *Ciudad Insigne y Siempre Leal de Manila* or "Distinguished and Ever Loyal City of Manila". The entire archipelago was named the Philippines (*Las Filipinas*), after the Spanish Crown Prince Philip who later became King Philip II. Henceforth, the island group experienced a history very different from most of the Malay Archipelago to which geographically, anthropologically and culturally it belonged. They saw the advent of colonialism only two centuries later.

From the very beginning, Manila and the Philippine islands were administered from New Spain, rather than from Spain itself, due to the immense distance between the two territories. As the capital city of the furthest-flung colony, Manila served primarily as a strategic entrepôt between China, America and Europe, and for two centuries it was the western terminus of a global trading route that spanned the Pacific and Atlantic oceans. Furthermore, when New Spain transitioned into independent Mexico in 1821, the Philippines benefitted even more. As the colony came under direct Spanish rule, it saw greater investment and immigration, and was able to develop into the fabled and fabulous "Pearl of the Orient" as described by 19th-century sailors.

Previous page: Fort Santiago during the American era.
Left, top to bottom: *Caribous in the sunset; sampan on the Pasig River, Manila; planting rice in the countryside.*

Below: The Malacanang Palace (1750).
Bottom: The Bridge of Spain (1875).
Right top: Engraving of a Spanish galleon circa 1580.
Right bottom: Model of a Spanish galleon in San Agustin Church.

The Manila Galleon Trade

For 250 years, Manila was one point of a global trade route that saw silks, porcelain and spices from China, Japan and the Spice Islands taken by a fleet of treasure ships thousands of miles across the Pacific to Acapulco in New Spain (present-day Mexico). There, they were transported by land to the port of Vera Cruz on the Atlantic coast, to be taken by another fleet to Europe. In return, European gold, silver and manufactured goods made the long and arduous journey back across two oceans and through New Spain to Manila, where they enriched the colonial proprietors of these exported luxury goods.

Trade was so profitable that only one to three galleons were needed to make the journey between Manila and Acapulco annually. In fact, for almost an entire century in the late 1700s and early 1800s, only a single galleon plied the Pacific route each year. However, the galleon trade was an exceedingly risky venture, not only because of the distance these ships had to travel – it took six months to travel across the Pacific! – but because the weather was frequently stormy and the waters hazardous, and, to top it all, the galleons were also the target of not just pirates, but British and Dutch naval fleets who besieged them if they could.

It is said that 100 such galleons didn't reach their destination, with many sinking on the way. Some have been excavated along the coasts of California, Guam or Saipan, but in general, most remain where they are, waiting to be discovered. This makes the Manila galleon trade one of the most tantalizing, yet-to-be-researched chapters of world history, and Manila, one of the most under-appreciated port cities today.

Intramuros

Manila's Walled City is a mediaeval teardrop-shaped fortress, dating from the 1590s, huddled by the banks of the Pasig River. To the north, across the river, is the fashionable district of Binondo, joined to it by the Bridge of Spain. It was where the Spanish colonialists settled locals and other resident aliens such as the Chinese. To the south is La Luñeta, known as Rizal Park today, and situated within a larger monumental precinct designed by the Americans.

In the 1590s, construction started on a series of extensive fortifications designed to protect the city of Manila and its Spanish colonial inhabitants not just from foreign invaders, but also from rebellious natives and residents. During the 16th to the 18th centuries, during which time Manila was understood to be the city that lay *intramuros* or "within the walls", fortification continued. This city-cum-citadel enclave housed the seat of the Spanish colonial government, religion and culture, as well as the homes of the Spanish. However, there weren't that many of them — being the farthest-flung colony, Manila never saw more than a few thousand colonials at any one time.

The walls themselves were 22 feet high and eight feet thick and were ringed by a deep moat. Entrance to the city was through eight gates, or *puertas*, the most imposing of which was Fort Santiago, on the northwest corner. Until the 1850s,

the drawbridges to these gates were raised at 11pm every evening, and lowered again at 4am the next morning. Those who lived *extramuros* or outside the walls — those natives and the Chinese traders who entered the city to serve as domestics or to do business with the Spaniards — had to leave the city every single day.

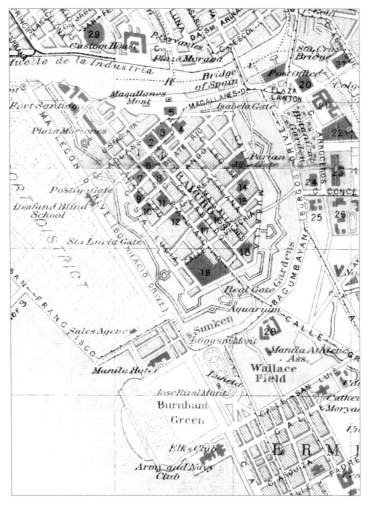

Historical accounts and archival photos reveal a surreal European landscape of Baroque churches and elegant courtyard houses; and of façades painted in Mediterranean shades of white, blue and ochre. Architecturally, Manila resembled the cities of South America, particularly Mexico City and Lima, Peru to which it had far closer ties than to any other city in the region.

Unfortunately, almost all the edifices within the walls were reduced to rubble in the aftermath of World War II — and remain a bewildering still-ruined landscape in an impoverished, post-independence Philippines today. Of the eight gates, only five remain; of the eight grand churches, only two. Nonetheless, walking through these tragically evocative ruins, re-colonised today by middle-income housing and squatter settlements, one can just about conjure up visions of sequestered and other-worldly splendour: Spanish *doñas* and their chamber-maids slipping into *calesas* or traditional horse-drawn carriages that still ply the walled city; the plaintive strains of a guitar as a *caballero* serenades a lover beneath her balcony with an old Andalucian love song; and the silent, stoic shuffle of Franciscan monks in their brown cowls, gathering for prayer and evensong in the city's massive Gothic cathedral.

Opposite left, top to bottom: The Parian Gate (1593); postcard of the Intramuros Wall; Fort Santiago today.
Opposite right: Interior of the San Agustin Church, a UNESCO World Heritage site.
Above left: The Ayuntamiento (Seat of the City Council, 1738).
Above right: Manila Cathedral (1879).
Left: Map of Manila depicting Intramuros and the Luñeta, 1917.

Extramuros

Above, left to right: Binondo Church (1852) and a calesa; Binondo Canal (early 1900s); the Pasig River in the early 1900s.
Opposite, clockwise from top: More scenes from the early 1900s — two views of the Calle de la Escolta; Plaza de Cervantes; Plaza Goiti and Calle de la Escolta.
Opposite, inset: Calle de la Escolta today.

By the mid 1800s, with the Philippines under direct Spanish rule, the colonial city had far outgrown the walls of Intramuros. The natural centre of the city had skipped over the walls to the adjacent neighborhood of Binondo, just across the Pasig River. Binondo was Manila's Chinatown, and also the oldest Chinatown in the world, having been established in 1594. It used to sit in direct aim of the cannons on the wall: a Chinese revolt in the early 1600s resulted in a massacre of more than 20,000 Chinese, and, henceforth, the Spanish took no chances.

From the mid 1800s until World War II, Binondo was the centre of trade, commerce, retail, finance and banking in Manila, and home to an entire new class of Chinese, as well as Chinese or Spanish *mestizos* (mixed-raced Filipinos). It became an immensely wealthy and beautiful precinct — with broad boulevards, townhouses in the traditional Spanish style, public plazas, a tramline and elegant churches, including the Binondo Church (established in 1596, but today's building dates from 1852).

The very heart of Binondo was Calle de la Escolta, the main shopping and commercial street, and the most fashonable place to be in the city — its Fifth Avenue, or Oxford Street, so to speak. Today, the street is still bustling, but it never recovered from a decline in the 1960s and '70s when the commercial district moved to the new suburb of Makati.

Imperial Ambition

Above: *Commodore Dewey at the Battle of Manila Bay, 1900.*
Opposite left, top to bottom: *Governor-General Wood at the Malacanang Palace; Fort Santiago; Manila's General Post Office today.*
Opposite right top: *Portrait of Dr. José Rizal.*
Opposite right bottom: *The Rizal Monument in the 1920s and today.*

On 23 April 1898, war was declared between Imperial Spain and the United States of America, when, in the aftermath of the Cuban revolution, the latter declared it would mobilize any military force necessary to intervene and assist Cuba's fight for independence from the former. The war soon escalated into a trans Atlantic and Pacific War, when the Philippines also erupted in revolution — and the U.S.A. again decided to intervene.

The obsolescent Spanish Empire was no match for the Americans and the Spanish-American War was won in only ten weeks. The 1898 Treaty of Paris sealed the end of the Spanish Empire, with the latter ceding Cuba, Puerto Rico, Guam and the Philippines to American rule. Initially allies to their Filipino counterparts fighting for independence, the Americans then turned the tables and annexed the country as American colonial territory, waging a bitter war — the Philippine-American War — to assert their hegemony.

The American colonial period, however, was brief — a mere 48 years from 1898 to 1946, when the Philippines finally won its independence in the aftermath of World War II. The colonial government, headed by Governor-General William Howard Taft (who eventually became the 17th President of the United States) initially drafted ambitious urban plans for a thoroughly rational, thoroughly American city to be built over the messy and mediaeval Spanish one. The architect and urban planner they commissioned was none other than Daniel Burnham, the man responsible for the urban plans of downtown Chicago and Washington D.C., as well as the architectural design for Union Station and the Flatiron Building in New York City.

But, except for a few major thoroughfares like Taft Avenue and Roxas Boulevard, as well as a dozen or so major civic and government buildings, most of the Burnham Plan was never executed, not least because of constant petitioning by Filipino leaders against American rule and for Philippine independence.

In the meantime, the Americans took over what the Spanish had left behind. The Malacanang Palace (1750), the residence of the Spanish Governor, became that of his American inheritors. Fort Santiago was refashioned as the Headquarters of the U.S. Army in the Philippines, and a new building was constructed just behind its centuries-old gate. The moat surrounding the Walled City — by then festering and filthy — was filled in with soil and turned into the Intramuros Golf Course. Other new edifices built in functional and monumental Neo-classical style include the Central Post Office Building (1926), the Manila Army and Navy Club (1911), the Elks Club (1911) which functioned as the centre of the American social circle, and the Manila Hotel (overleaf), all of which still stand today.

The Martyrdom of Dr. José Rizal

It is impossible to give an account of Manila's history without that of its National Hero, Dr. José Rizal, the man who played a pivotal role in ending Spanish colonial rule and securing Philippine Independence (by way of a brief and transitional American colonial period).

In 1887, fresh from his medical studies at the Central University of Madrid, Spain, Rizal published the first of his two famous novels — *Noli Me Tangere* (*Touch Me Not*). In it, he vilified the Spanish ruling class, exposing the widespread corruption not just within the ranks of government, but also within the clergy. Soon after the book's publication, it was banned in the Philippines and Rizal was branded a subversive by the Spanish colonial authorities.

However, by 1892, *Noli Me Tangere* was widely known amongst intellectuals in the Philippines, and the book, coupled with Rizal's forced exile from the capital, indirectly gave rise to a militant civic movement that called for independence from the Spanish. When this movement imploded into full-scale revolution in 1896, Rizal was doomed. Despite professing a distaste for violence and distancing himself from the revolution, Rizal was recalled from exile, charged for treason, tried, and summarily executed.

More than a century later, Rizal continues to be revered and commemorated religiously in Manila. Fort Santiago, the ancient fortified entrance to Intramuros, houses the Rizal Shrine, a museum that documents his history from cradle to grave. His execution spot, once a public park known by the Spanish as La Luñeta (1820) but now called Rizal Park houses a giant monument to the man himself and a mausoleum where his mortal remains are interred and guarded 24/7 by two "Knights of Rizal". Finally, for the truly devoted, Rizal Park also offers the Diorama of the Martyrdom of Dr. José Rizal, an interactive light and sound presentation that re-enacts, in graphic detail and with lasers and other special effects, Rizal's entire experience of martyrdom, from arrest to imprisonment to execution.

A Grand American Hotel

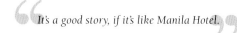

Even in the remotest corners of the globe, the name Manila Hotel is a symbol of hotel excellence—it is the Manila home of important personages from all parts of the world.

The Manila Hotel attracts the discriminating patronage of local residents and visitors alike. The distinguished atmosphere, the impeccable service and the matchless cuisine of this famous and modern hotel are a delightful revelation to world travelers who visit our shores.

Every convenience and luxury is incorporated for the comfort and pleasure of our thousands of yearly guests and our greatest recommendation comes from those who have made the Manila Hotel their headquarters in the Philippines. They know, and they tell their friends.

"IT'S THE PLACE TO GO"

The Manila Hotel

Your Guarantee of Safety and Sanitation in the Tropics

H. C. ("ANDY") ANDERSON, *Managing Director*

Cable Address: MANHOCO, MANILA

In its heyday in the early 1900s, the Manila Hotel was considered one of the grandest hotels in the East. It was established in 1912 to cater to the thousands of American tourists who flocked to the Philippines after it became American sovereign territory in 1898.

In its original form, the hotel was a five-storey, all-suite affair designed in the California Mission style with clean lines, simple aesthetics, and a kind of understated elegance. Sitting on the edge of Manila Bay, its eye-catching green roof and white façade signified a welcome sight for weary travellers arriving by sea from the distant ports of the U.S.A..

Today, the original hotel building still exists, but is now dwarfed by an 18-storey tower affixed to the hotel during an extensive overhaul and expansion commissioned by Imelda Marcos in the '70s. Whether arriving at the International Cruise Terminal in Manila Bay, cruising along Roxas Boulevard, or strolling within the walls of Intramuros, the tower, with the words "MANILA HOTEL" emblazoned boldly in gold, is impossible to miss.

The interior of the hotel now sports a sort of over-the-top Hollywood opulence with Filipino flair. Once past the glass doors (and tight security screening), it is hard not to be arrested by the vastness and theatricality of the lobby space, apparently the largest hotel lobby in the world: an expanse of Philippine hardwood, marble and other gleaming materials.

The old lobby has been relegated to an ante-lobby, and only in that coolly whitewashed space can the visitor imagine how the hotel was in its initial years, with those 1920s' American ladies bursting dramatically onto the scene in their flapper dresses and hats, smiling at the sailors that swaggered through the hotel's doors in their uniforms, looking to have a good time.

Besides Ernest Hemingway, the Manila Hotel has seen its own share of the rich and famous in its 100-year existence. Among the staying guests were Charlton Heston, Marlon Brando, Dame Margot Fonteyn, Richard Nixon and even The Beatles, who famously came through Manila, refused an invite to (Imelda) Marcos' Presidential Palace, and declared how they hated the city. But, most important of them all, was General Douglas MacArthur, the man who accepted the surrender of the Japanese and thus ended World War II in the Pacific. The general lived in a specially commissioned "Presidential" Suite of the hotel for six years until just before the outbreak of war. Today, the hotel maintains a suite dedicated to the general containing a collection of MacArthur memorabilia.

Opposite top: Manila Hotel's luggage label.
Opposite bottom: Advertisement for Manila Hotel, 1930s.
Above: Manila Hotel seen from the water, 1930s.
Right: Manila Hotel's entrance today.

Hong Kong

"*Mad dogs and Englishmen go out in the midday sun.*
The smallest Malay rabbit deplores this foolish habit.
In Hong Kong they strike a gong and fire off a noonday gun…"

— Noel Coward, *Mad Dogs and Englishmen* (1932)

Fragrant Harbour

Geographically and politically, Hong Kong occupies the midway point between maritime South East Asia and the vast, exotic mainland of China. A mere one degree in latitude north of Hanoi, and many degrees south of the northern boundaries of Burma and Vietnam, Hong Kong was an obligatory stop on the Grand Tour whether one's destination was distant Yokohama in Japan, or across the Pacific Ocean to California.

The history of the city began in the aftermath of the First Opium War, when Chinese authorities burnt more than 20,000 chests of opium imported by British merchants through the port city of Canton, and chased Her Majesty's merchants out of the city. In retaliation, British troops occupied the island of Hong Kong, at the mouth of the Pearl River, in 1841. A year later, the Treaty of Nanking ceded the island to the British in perpetuity; and five other Chinese cities — Canton, Amoy, Foochow, Ningpo and Shanghai — were forced open as Treaty Ports to international (i.e. European) trade.

During the latter part of the 19th century, Hong Kong acquired more territory: The 1860 Convention of Peking, signed in the aftermath of the Second Opium War, ceded the Kowloon peninsula to the British on the same terms as Hong Kong island; and, in 1898, the Second Convention of Peking allowed the colonial authorities to lease for a period

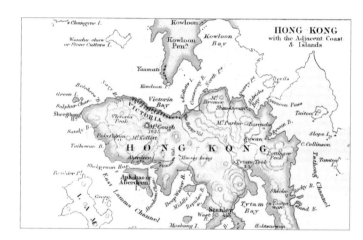

of 99 years, rent-free, the rest of the Kowloon peninsula, known thereafter as the New Territories. That lease period was inevitably applied to the rest of Hong Kong as well.

Hong Kong, like its sister city Singapore before it, was governed as a Crown Colony, with a Governor appointed by the British Queen (or King). As a free port, it allowed merchant ships from all over the world to dock and trade their wares without paying duties. As such, it became a rich and prosperous emporium-city, one of the last of its kind in the colonial era, and gained somewhat of a reputation as a heady and hedonistic "Wild West" frontier town in the Far East. Inevitably, in 1997, it was "handed over" as a Special Administrative Territory to the People's Republic of China.

Previous page: View down Des Voeux Road, early 1900s.
Top: St. John's Cathedral, set against skyscrapers in Central.
Top right: Map of Hong Kong island and Kowloon Peninsula, 1900s.

Opposite left below and far right:
The iconic Victoria Harbour. This narrow sliver of water between Hong Kong Island and Kowloon was fed by fresh water, which explains why the name of the city translates as "Fragrant Harbour" — the streams of fresh water from Kowloon were "fragrant".

Above: Hong Kong's waterfront, early 1900s.

Right: Statue Square, with Prince's Building (1904) to the left, Queen's Building (1899) to the right and the statue of Queen Victoria (1887) at centre.

Hong Kong Island

The beating heart of the colony was Hong Kong Island, a mere 80 square km of land often referred to as "the rock". Indeed, in the early days, it was nothing more than a collection of colonial edifices clinging precariously to a steep mountainous outcrop.

To the north of the island, facing Kowloon on mainland China, was Victoria Harbour, a natural, deep-water bay. For more than 100 years, the harbour played host to a magnificent parade of ships from all over the world. Today, the port of Hong Kong is still located here and is one of the busiest in the world. Its backdrop, however, is much changed, with most of Hong Kong's older Palladian and Italianate buildings being replaced by towering skyscrapers that comprise the engine for one of the world's foremost financial capitals.

Immediately south of the harbour sits the old colonial city of Victoria, now known simply as Central. Aside from San Francisco, it is probably the most vertigo-inducing urban area in the world, because the British literally built wherever they managed to gain a foothold on the mountainous slopes. Then, as now, Central was the city's administrative and financial core, housing both government offices and the headquarters of multi-national merchant houses, banks and other financial institutions. At its heart is Statue Square, known for a statue of Queen Victoria that used to sit in the middle of the square but was removed during the Japanese Occupation to a park in Causeway Bay. Around the square stood (and still stand) some of the city's most important and magnificent institutions

Above: *Chinese junks at the Hong Kong harbour.*
Right: *The Hong Kong harbour today.*
Far right: *The British fleet in Hong Kong harbour.*
Opposite left, top and middle: *The former Supreme Court Building (1914) is today's Legislative Council Building. LegCo (as it is known) is the one-chamber legislature of the Hong Kong Special Administrative Region.*
Opposite left, bottom: *The Central Magistracy building (1914).*

— the former Supreme Court Building (today's Legislative Council Building, 1912); City Hall (1869); the Hong Kong Club (1897); and the offices of the Hong Kong and Shanghai Banking Corporation (1886). With the exception of the Supreme Court Building, all of these have been replaced with modernist, contemporary structures — most notably Sir Norman Foster's iconic H.S.B.C. tower — and the square itself is overshadowed by a plethora of towering skyscrapers that make up Hong Kong's International Financial Centre.

The other unique feature of Central is its maze of colonial-era streets, which still retain their original names and largely ply the very same route they did when laid out. The most famous street is Queen's Road (1842), the very first street laid down in the city. This bisects the whole of Central, running east from the racecourse at Happy Valley through to the Chinese quarters in Sheung Wan. Queen's Road, housing the most fashionable shops and restaurants, was the centre of commerce and retail in the colony; it is also where one finds Hong Kong's iconic tramline, introduced in 1904 and still operating today.

Unfortunately, most of the colonial-era buildings, and the history that surrounded them, have long since vanished. What remains today — and this is true of Hong Kong in general — are a scattering of largely religious or peripheral institutions, some-how forgotten in the city's race to develop. Like Statue Square, all these relics from the past stand surrounded by and somewhat lost within the vertical city that Hong Kong has become.

South of Central, dominating all views of Hong Kong's skyline, is Victoria Peak, Hong Kong's other major landmark. Better known simply as the Peak, it is the highest point of elevation on Hong Kong island, rising at about 1,800 feet above sea level. The Peak was the foremost residential address for the European élite and was scattered with opulent mansions, reminiscent of aristocratic homes in the English countryside. Initially, access to the Peak was a major barrier as there were only two ways up — the first by foot along the steep incline of Old Peak Road, the second by sedan chair, hoisted aloft by two or sometimes four coolies. The introduction of the Peak Tramway in 1888, a major innovation in public transport technology at the time, transformed all that.

Today, the Peak continues to be Hong Kong's most exclusive address, with the resident Chinese élite largely replacing their British counterparts and completely modernising the landscape. Even though most of the major landmarks have been demolished, the Peak Tram still remains, shuttling hundreds of passengers up the slopes in under five minutes every day. A highlight of any visit up the slopes are the magnificent views of Hong Kong harbour — views that have amazed residents and visitors alike for as long as Hong Kong has existed.

This page: *Various modes of public transportation including the Peak Tram in the 1900s (above); the cable car (right top); the Peak Tram today (right middle); and the Queen Street Tram in the 1930s (right bottom).*
Opposite: *Views of Hong Kong harbour from the Peak today and in the early 1900s (inset).*

The British in Hong Kong

From the beginning till the end of Hong Kong's colonial period, the British were far outnumbered on their own home turf, numbering less than five percent of the total population in the early 1900s and less than one percent post World War II. They occupied a narrow stratum at the very top of colonial society within which there were further class divisions. At the highest echelons of British society, and more powerful than any other persons in Hong Kong, save the Governor, were the *taipans* (pronounced "dai-ban" in Cantonese, and meaning "big boss"). These were the heads of the major multi-national trading firms, banks and other companies headquartered in the colony: Jardine,

Matheson & Co., Butterfield & Swire, Dent & Co., the Hong Kong & Shanghai Banking Corporation, and so on.

The *taipans* and their families resided on the Peak, alongside other wealthy and influential Europeans such as diplomats, senior colonial officials and socialites. Up in these Olympian heights, they held opulent balls, dinner parties and soirées overlooking the rest of Hong Kong and the South China Sea. A retinue of domestic servants both Chinese and Indian waited on them, while their children were taken care of by Chinese *amahs*, or nursemaids.

Junior colonial officials and employees of the major companies who could not afford to live on the Peak occupied

the area known as Mid-Levels alongside the wealthier Chinese. In those days, access to Mid-Levels was also arduous, requiring passage by sedan chair or rickshaw. Today, Mid-levels is connected to Central by yet another innovative and iconic means of public conveyance — an escalator.

Centres of social activity in the colony included various clubs and associations, of which there were more than a dozen, including the most prestigious of them all, the Hong Kong Club, with its cricket grounds facing the harbour. Weekends and special occasions saw the fashionable set descending upon the famous racecourse in Happy Valley (built in 1845 and still in existence), to cheer and bet on their favourite horses while decked out in their best hats, dresses and suits.

Opposite top left: *Seal of the Hong Kong & Shanghai Banking Corporation.*
Opposite below, left to right: *Various residences on Victoria Peak; the Hong Kong Club (1897), designed by Palmer & Turner; British gentleman in a rickshaw, the Peak, early 1900s.*
This page: *Happy Valley Racecourse today and in the early 1900s (inset).*

Kowloon and Beyond

The name Kowloon translates as "Nine Dragons". A legend from the 12th century AD has it that, when the last Emperor of the Sung Dynasty fled from rampaging Mongol hordes as a mere boy, he was brought here to this barren corner of China to be hidden away. The nine dragons were the eight peaks the boy emperor counted as he stood at the edge of the peninsula, with the ninth dragon being himself. He would later jump to his death from the same peak when the Mongols finally found him.

After Kowloon was ceded to the British in 1860 it was used largely as a defensive barrier against the Chinese. Later, because of its proximity to Hong Kong island, it was developed into the colony's transport hub, housing the city's naval base and Marine Police Headquarters (1884), the terminal station of the Canton-Kowloon Railway (1910), and from 1925 to 1998, the city's first international airport Kai Tak. The latter, surrounded by mountains and high-rises, was known by pilots to be fiendishly difficult to land at.

Today, Kowloon is one of the most densely populated districts in Hong Kong, and the centre of Hong Kong Chinese culture. The edge of the peninsula, known as Tsim Sha Tsui (meaning "Sharp Sandy Mouth"), is home to a number of luxury malls, the Peninsula Hotel (see pages 202–205) and some of the most fashionable retail outlets in the city. It is also where one still finds most of the area's remaining pieces of British colonial heritage, particularly in the immediate vicinity of the Star Ferry terminal, and along both sides of Nathan Road, the main thoroughfare.

Left, top: *The clock tower of the former Canton-Kowloon Railway Station was preserved and incorporated into the Hong Kong Cultural Centre complex.*
Left, middle: *The former Marine Police Headquarters, now converted into a hotel and retail establishment.*
Left bottom: *Kowloon Union Church (1927).*
Right: *Kowloon, early 1900s.*
Opposite: *View of Kowloon harbour, early 1900s (top); the Star Ferry in the early 1900s and little changed today (below).*

The Star Ferry

Besides that of a Chinese junk, the image of the Star Ferry set against the skyline is one of the most iconic portraits of Hong Kong. Plying between Central and Kowloon, the ferry was the brainchild of a resident merchant of Parsee ethnicity, Mr. Dorabjee Nowrojee, and commenced operations in 1888. Even though the journey is shorter today, it is still in service. Passengers wishing to cross from Hong Kong island to Kowloon, or vice versa, pay from just HK$2 for the seven-minute ride and the spectacular views of the harbour.

Above: Kowloon Signal Hill and Tower, early 1900s.

Right top to bottom: Kowloon Cricket Club (1904) today; a residential apartment in Kowloon today; the Signal Tower at the Marine Police Headquarters — its time ball apparatus was moved to Signal Hill in 1907.

Opposite, clockwise from top: Chinese quarter along Queen's Road Central; Chinese ladies playing cards; wealthy Chinese gentlemen being carried in a rickshaw and sedan chair; the tanka, or boat people in Aberdeen Harbour.

Kowloon was also known for its walled city, which remained under Chinese jurisdiction even after the British occupied Kowloon. A traditional Chinese city in all senses, it was a highly dense settlement encircled by a wall. In the 1970s, taking advantage of the ambiguous jurisdiction and the ensuing lack of building laws, the Walled City gradually evolved into a high-rise slum, populated with thousands of Chinese families and micro-businesses crammed into a 2.7 hectare space. Largely Triad controlled, it was a notorious black market, trafficking everything from fake Rolexes to (it is said) human organs. The site was cleared finally in the '80s and today it houses a park.

Kowloon is the southern-most point of a larger peninsula known as the New Territories, leased to Britain in 1898 for 100 years — a lease term which would eventually be applied to Kowloon proper and Hong Kong Island as well. Then and now, the New Territories is a largely rustic and rural landscape, with scenic trails through verdant mountainside, interspersed with some of the last remaining true village communities in one of the most urbanised spaces on earth.

Above: *The Peninsula Hong Kong today, with its fleet of 14 Rolls-Royce Phantoms.*
Right and far right: *Two views of the Peninsula Hong Kong in the 1930s.*
Opposite left: *Portrait of Elly, Lawrence and Horace Kadoorie, the founders and owners of the Peninsula Hong Kong (left) and the hotel's famous page boys in white livery, from an advertising campaign, "Portraits of Peninsula" featuring images by Annie Leibowitz (right).*
Opposite far right: *Postcard from the hotel depicting traditional Chinese door deities (top); advertisement for the hotel, 1930s (below).*

The Peninsula Hong Kong

The Peninsula Hong Kong is the youngest hotel on this Grand Tour, just as Hong Kong itself is its youngest colony. Opened in 1928, it is the flagship property of the Peninsula Group. This in turn is undersigned by Hongkong and Shanghai Hotels Limited, a holding company responsible for some of the most famous hotels in China, including the former Hotel de Wagon-Lits in Peking, the Astor House Hotel and Palace Hotel in Shanghai, and the former Peak Hotel and Repulse Bay Hotel in Hong Kong. The man behind the Peninsula was Sir Lawrence Kadoorie, a British *taipan* of Jewish origin, who had intended for the Peninsula to be the finest and most modern hotel East of Suez. The Kadoorie family continues to hold the majority stake in the Peninsula and its holding company today.

The Peninsula Hong Kong was constructed at the height of the glory days of travel, just before the Great Depression struck. At the time, Kowloon was developing into a major transport hub, with the Tsim Sha Tsui area fronting the harbour being the terminus where ocean liners bearing passengers on Far Eastern or round-the-world cruises docked. Similarly, the Canton-Kowloon railway station, the terminus for passengers who travelled overland from Europe via the Trans-Siberian Railway, was nearby. The Peninsula Hong Kong was thus built to ensure sufficient luxury accommodation for the hundreds of tourists that were arriving in Hong Kong, via Kowloon

Designed by the architect, W. D. Goodfellow, of Hong Kong Realty and Trust, the hotel was a six-storey building, with 160 guest rooms fitted with their own suite bathrooms. The highlight of the hotel was its expansive lobby on the ground floor; designed in an Italian Renaissance style, it featured soaring, fluted columns and intricate, gilt-framed gargoyle faces.

The Peninsula Hong Kong quickly became the social centre of the colony's élite, playing host to celebrities, *taipans*,

This page: The Peninsula Hong Kong's grand lobby today (inset) and in the 1930s (right).

royalty and heads of state. However, being built so late in the game, it also could not escape the effects of social upheaval in China and soon after, the Japanese Occupation. The hotel's star really began to rise post-war, when Shanghai was lost to Mao Tse-tung's new China, and Hong Kong became the bastion of Western culture and capitalism.

Today's Peninsula Hong Kong is a product of this post-war growth and reconsolidation. The iconic pageboys in white livery were introduced in the 1950s; the sleek fleet of equally iconic Rolls Royces in the 1970s. Finally, in 1994,

a new 30-storey Tower Wing, adding 132 guest rooms as well as spectacular views of the Hong Kong skyline, was inaugurated. Despite these changes, the hotel manages to maintain an air of the glory days of travel in the 1920s and '30s. This is particularly evoked at the world-famous high tea set in the warm and enveloping expanse of the lobby. As guests sample an immaculately prepared array of scones, pastries and sandwiches, from somewhere up high a resident string quartet strikes up a medley of waltzes and light music, thereby re-creating an atmosphere of bygone days.

Clockwise from top left: The share-holders of the Peninsula Hong Kong, 1930s; the driveway and entrance to the Peninsula today; The Peninsula's fleet of Rolls-Royce Silver Shadows, 1970s.

Acknowledgements

The author wishes to express his deepest appreciation to everyone who has made this book possible – in particular, Ian, Kim, Norreha, Chee Ying, Stephy, Janice and the team at Talisman. Special thanks go to Mr. John Koh, for the use of pieces from his inspiring collection, and for opening the author's mind up to the history and heritage of travel. Thanks go also to friends and colleagues at the National Museum of Singapore, the Singapore Philatelic Museum and the National Heritage Board of Singapore for the unflinching support, advice and assistance rendered in the author's search for archival material. Finally, the author owes a big debt of gratitude to Joe for his infinite patience.

The publisher wishes to acknowledge and offer sincere thanks to the Estate of our late colleague Luca Invernizzi Tettoni (1949–2013) for permission to use numerous images from his archive in the production of this book.

Reference and Further Reading

Southeast Asia and Travel

- Artmonsky, Ruth and Cox, Susie, 2012. *P & O — Across the Oceans, Across the Years*. UK: Antique Collectors' Club.
- Beeson, Mark (Ed.), 2004. *Contemporary Southeast Asia*. Second Edition. UK: Palgrave Macmillan.
- Berneron-Couvenhes, Marie-Françoise, 2007. *Les Messageries Maritimes – L'essor d'une grande compagnie de navigation française, 1851 – 1894*. Paris: Presses de l'Université Paris-Sorbonne.
- Bird, Isabella, 1883. *The Golden Chersonese and the Way Thither*. 2010 Digital Edition. New York: Cambridge University Press.
- Crawfurd, John, 1830. *Journal of an Embassy to the Courts of Siam and Cochin-China, exhibiting a view of the actual State of these Kingdoms*. Google Books Digital Edition. London.
- Deakes, Christopher and Stanley, Tom, 2013. *A Century of Sea Travel – Personal Accounts from the Steamship Era*. Great Britain: Seaforth Publishing.
- Fletcher, R. A., 1913. *Travelling Palaces: Luxury in Passenger Steamships*. London: Sir Isaac Pitman & Sons, Ltd.
- Fletcher, R. A., 1910. *Steamships – the Story of their Development to the Present Day*. London: Sidgwick & Jackson, Ltd.
- Kipling, Rudyard, 1892. "Mandalay." From *Barrack-Room Ballads, and Other Verses*. London: Methuen Publishing.
- Lockard, Craig A., 2009. *Southeast Asia in World History*. UK: Oxford University Press.
- Maugham, W. Somerset, 1926. *The Casuarina Tree*. London: Heinemann, London.
- Maugham, W. Somerset, 1930. *The Gentleman in the Parlour: A Record of a Journey from Rangoon to Haiphong*. 2001 New Edition. London: Vintage Books.
- Meade, Martin, Fitchett, J. and Lawrence, A., 1987. *Grand Oriental Hotels: From Cairo to Tokyo, 1800 – 1939*. London: J. M. Dent & Sons.
- Osbourne, Milton, 2013. *Southeast Asia – An Introductory History*. 11th Edition. Australia: Allen & Unwin.
- Ricklefs, M.C. et al, 2010. *A New History of Southeast Asia*. UK: Palgrave MacMillan, UK.
- Wallace, Alfred Russell, 1869. *The Malay Archipelago – The Land of the Orang-Utan, and the Bird of Paradise*. 1989 Edition. Singapore: Oxford University Press.

Rangoon

- Augustin, Andreas, 2001. *The Strand Treasury* (E-Book). The Most Famous Hotels in the World.
- Aung San, Suu Kyi, 1991. *Freedom from Fear and Other Writings*. 2010 Edition. London: Penguin Books.
- Aung-Thwin, Michael and Aung-Thwin, Maitrii, 2012. *A History of Myanmar Since Ancient Times: Traditions and Transformations*. Second Edition. London: Reaktion Books.
- Charney, Michael W, 2009. *A History of Modern Burma*. UK: Cambridge University Press.
- Kelly, Robert Talbot, 1908. *Burma: Peeps At Many Lands*. London: A. & C. Black.
- Orwell, George, 1934. *Burmese Days*. UK: Oxford City Press.
- Singer, Noel F., 1995. *Old Rangoon – City of the Shwedagon*. Scotland: Paul Strachan – Kiscadale Publications.

Penang

- Andaya, Barbara W. and Andaya, Leonard Y., 2001. *A History of Malaysia*. Second Edition. UK: Palgrave.
- Barber, Andrew, 2009. *Penang under the East India Company, 1786 – 1858*. Malaysia: AB & A.
- Bilainkin, George, 1932. *Hail Penang! – Being the Narrative of Comedies and Tragedies in a Tropical Outpost, among Europeans, Chinese, Malays, and Indians*. 2010 Edition. Areca Reprints, Penang.
- Cheah, Jin Seng, 2012. *Penang – 500 Early Postcards*. Singapore: Editions Didier Millet.
- Flower, Raymond, 2009. *The Penang Adventure: A History of the Pearl of the Orient*. Singapore: Marshall Cavendish Editions.
- Hoyt, Sarnia Hayes, 1991. *Old Penang*. Singapore: Oxford University Press.
- Moore, Wendy Khadijah, 2004. *Malaysia: A Pictorial History, 1400 – 2004*. Kuala Lumpur: Editions Didier Millet.
- Sharp, Ilsa, 2008. *The E & O Hotel – Pearl of Penang*. Singapore: Marshal Cavendish Editions.
- Shennan, Margaret, 2010. *Out in the Midday Sun: The British in Malaya, 1880 – 1960*. London: John Murray (Publishers) Ltd, London.

Malacca

- de Camões, Luis, 1572. *The Lusiads (Os Lusiadas)*. Translated by William Julius Mickles (1773). Project Gutenberg Edition. Lisbon.
- Hoyt, Sarnia Hayes, 1993. *Old Malacca*. Kuala Lumpur: Oxford University Press.
- Pires, Tomé, 1512 – 1515. *Suma Oriental: An Account of the East, from the Red Sea to China, written in Malacca and India in 1512 – 1515*. New Delhi: Asian Educational Services.
- Singh Sandhu, Kernial & Wheatley, Paul, 1983. *Melaka – The Transformation of a Malay Capital c. 1400 – 1980. Vols I and II*. Singapore: Institute of Southeast Asian Studies and Oxford University Press.
- Tun Sri Lanang, 1612. *Sejarah Melayu (The Malay Annals)*. Translated by Dr. John Leyden, 1821. Kuala Lumpur: Silverfish Malaysian Classics.
- de Sousa Pinto, Paulo Jorge, 2012. *The Portuguese and the Straits of Malacca, 1575 – 1619*. Translated by Roopanjali Roy. Singapore: National University of Singapore Press.
- Wong, Yunn Chii, 2011. *Historic Malacca Post Cards*. Singapore: Tun Tan Cheng Lock Centre for Asian Architectural and Urban Heritage.

Singapore

- Flower, Raymond, 1984. *Raffles – The Story of Singapore*. 2007 Edition. Singapore: Marshall Cavendish Editions.
- Frost, Mark Ravinder & Balasinghamchow, Yu-mei, 2010. *Singapore – A Biography*. Hong Kong: Hong Kong University Press.
- Glendinning, Victoria, 2012. *Raffles and the Golden Opportunity*. London: Profile Books.
- Kwa, Chong Guan, Heng, Derek and Tan, Tai Yong, 2009. *Singapore, A 700-Year History – From Early Emporium to World City*. Singapore: National Archives of Singapore.
- Manley, Iain, 2010. *Tales of Old Singapore – The Glorious Past of Asia's Greatest Emporium*. Hong Kong: Earnshaw Books.
- Liu, Gretchen, 1999. *Singapore – A Pictorial History, 1819 – 2000*. Singapore: National Heritage Board and Editions Didier Millet.
- Liu, Gretchen. *Raffles Hotel, 2006*. 2006 Edition. Singapore: Landmark Books.
- Raffles, Sir Thomas Stamford, 1819. "Letter to British East India Company, June 15th."
- Turnbull, C. M., 2009. *A History of Modern Singapore: 1819 – 2005*. Singapore: National University Press.
- Yeoh, Brenda, 1996. *Contesting Space: Power Relations and the Urban Built Environment in Singapore*. New York: Oxford University Press.

Reference and Further Reading, ctd.

Batavia

- Bosma, Ulbe and Raben, Remco, 2008. *Being "Dutch" in the Indies: A History of Creolisation and Empire, 1500 – 1920*. Singapore: National University of Singapore Press.
- Hannigan, Tim, 2012. *Raffles and the British Invasion of Java*. Singapore: Monsoon Books.
- Jayapal, Maya, 1993. *Old Jakarta*. Kuala Lumpur: Oxford University Press.
- Merrilees, Scott, 2000. *Batavia in Nineteenth Century Photographs*. Singapore: Editions Didier Millet.
- Merrilees, Scott, 2012. *Greetings from Jakarta: Postcards of a Capital 1900 – 1950*. Jakarta: Equinox Publishing.
- Niewenhuys, Robert (E. Breton de Nijs), 1954. *Faded Portraits*. 1999 Edition. Singapore: Periplus Editions.
- Raffles, Sir Thomas Stamford, 1817. *The History of Java*. 1994 Oxford in Asia Hardback Reprints Edition. Kuala Lumpur: Oxford University Press.
- Ricklefs, M.C., 1981. *A History of Modern Indonesia since c. 1200*. Fourth Edition. New York: Palgrave-Macmillan.
- Taylor, Jean Gelman, 1983. *The Social World of Batavia – European and Eurasians in Dutch Asia*. USA: University of Wisconsin Press.
- de Wit, Augusta, 1912. *Java – Facts and Fancies*. 1985 Edition. Singapore: Oxford University Press.

Soerabaja

- Asia Maior, 2004. *Soerabaja, 1900 – 1950 – Port, Navy, Townscape*. Zieriksee: Uitgeverij Asia Maior.
- Couperus, Louis, 1900. *The Hidden Force (De Stille Kracht)*. London: Quartet Books.
- Hannigan, Tim, *Articles on Old Surabaya*. Available at: http://tahannigan.blogspot.sg/2011/04/wandering-into-past-in-old-surabaya.html
- Multatuli, 1860. *Max Havelaar, or The Coffee Auctions of a Dutch Trading Company*. London: Penguin Classics.
- Nieuwenhuys, Robert, 1972. *Mirror of the Indies (Oost-Indische Spiegel)*. 1999 English edition translated by Frans van Rosevelt. Singapore: Periplus Editions.
- du Perron, Edgar, 1935. *Country of Origin (Het land van herkomst)*. 1999 Edition. Singapore: Periplus Editions.
- Toer, Pramoedya Ananta, 1980 - 1988. *The Buru Quartet*. In 4 volumes. Translated by Max Lane. New York: Penguin Books.

Bangkok

- Augustin, Andreas and Williamson, Andrew, 1996 – 2006. *The Oriental Bangkok*. The Most Famous Hotels in the World.
- Baker, Chris and Phongpaichit, Pasut, 2005. *A History of Thailand*. Third Edition. Australia: Cambridge University Press.
- Burslem, Chris, 2012. *Tales of Old Bangkok: Rich Stories From the Land of the White Elephant*. Malaysia: Earnshaw Books.
- Conrad, Joseph, 1900. *Lord Jim*. Project Gutenberg Edition.
- Conrad, Joseph, 1917. *The Shadow-Line: A Confession*. Project Gutenberg Edition.
- Landon, Margaret, 1944. *Anna and the King of Siam*. New York: Harper Perennial.
- Leonowens, Anna, 1870. *The English Governess at the Siamese Court*. London: Trubner and Co.

- O'Neil, Maryvelma, 2008. *Bangkok: A Cultural and Literary History*. Oxford: Signal Books.
- Tuck, Patrick, 1995. *The French Wolf and the Siamese Lamb – The French Threat to Siamese Independence, 1858 – 1907*. Bangkok: White Lotus Co., Ltd.
- Waugh, Alex, 1970. *Bangkok: The Story of a City*. London: Eland.

Saigon

- Brocheux, Pierre and Hémery, Daniel, 2009. *Indochina – An Ambiguous Colonization, 1858-1954*. Berkeley: University of California Press.
- Duras, Marguerite, 1984. *The Lover (L'Amant)*. Paris: Editions de Minuit.
- Friends of Vietnam Heritage, 2008. *Vignettes of French Culture in Hanoi*. Hanoi – The Gioi Publishers.
- Greene, Graham, 1955. *The Quiet American*. London: Penguin Classics Deluxe Edition.
- Karnow, Stanley, 1983. *Vietnam – A History*. London: Pimlico.
- Mallet / Toudy, 2014. *Saïgon / Vietnam*. Website. Available at: www.saigon.vietnam.free.fr/menu-saigon.php.
- Nguyen, Khac Vien & Huu, Ngoc, Ed, 1998. *From Saigon to Ho Chi Minh City – A Path of 300 Years*. Hanoi: The Gioi Publishers.
- Osbourne, Milton, 2000. *Mekong*. 2006 Updated Edition. Australia: Allen & Unwin.
- Sarraut, Albert, 1930. *Indochine*. Paris: Librairie de Paris, Firmin Didot et CIE.
- Scott, Parn, 2010. *In Search of the Pearl of the Far East: Sai Gon – Ho Chi Minh City*. Vietnam: The Gioi Publishers.
- Swain, Joe, 1996. *River of Time: A Memoir of Vietnam*. USA: Vintage.
- Triaire, Marguerite, 1944. *Indochina Through Texts*. 2000 English Edition. Hanoi: The Gioi Publishers.
- Wargnier, Régis, 1992. *Indochine*. Paris: Bac Films.

Phnom Penh

- Chandler, David, 2008. *A History of Cambodia*. USA: Westview Press.
- Higham, Charles, 2001. *The Civilisation of Angkor*. Great Britain: Phoenix.
- Igout, Michel, 1993. *Phnom Penh Then and Now*. Bangkok: White Lotus Co. Ltd.
- Jeldres, Julio A. & Chaijitvanit, Somkid, 1999. *The Royal Palace of Phnom Penh and Cambodian Royal Life*. Bangkok: Post Books.
- Loti, Pierre, 1912. *A Pilgrimage to Angkor (Un Pèlerin d'Angkor)*. 2012 Edition. Bangkok: Silkword Books.
- Malraux, André, 1930. *The Royal Way (La Voie Royale)*. 1961 Edition. New York: Random House.
- Montague, Joel G., 2010. *Picture Postcards of Cambodia, 1900 – 1950*. Bangkok: White Lotus Press.
- Tully, John, 2002. *France on the Mekong – A History of the Protectorate in Cambodia, 1863 – 1953*. USA: University Press of America.

Hanoi

- Augustin, Andreas, 2012. *Sofitel Legend Metropole Hotel*. The Most Famous Hotels in the World.
- Cunningham, Alfred, 1902. *The French in Tonkin & South Asia*. 2013 Edition. London: Forgotten Books.
- Logan, William S., 2000. *Hanoi – Biography of a City*. Singapore: Select Publishing.
- Nguyen, Dinh-Hoa, 1999. *From Inside the Red River: a Cultural Memoir of*

Mid-century Vietnam. NC: MacFarland & Company, New York.
- Nguyen, Manh Hung, (Ed.), 2009. *Hanoi Xua – Hanoi in Ancient Time*. Saigon: Nha Xuat Ban Van Hoa Sai Gon.
- Nguyen, Thua Hy, 2002. *Economic History of Hanoi in the 17th, 18th and 19th Centuries*. English translation edited by Barbara Cohen. Hanoi: National Political Publishing House.
- Sidel, Mark, 1998. *Old Hanoi*. Singapore: Oxford University Press.
- Sontag, Susan, 1969. *Trip to Hanoi*. New York: Farrar, Straus and Giroux.
- Wintle, Justin, 1991. *Romancing Vietnam: Inside the Boat Country*. Oxford: Signal Books Limited.

Manila

- Fish, Shirley, 2011. The *Manila-Acapulco Galleons: The Treasure Ships of the Pacific*. UK: Authorhouse.
- Francia, Luis, 2010. *A History of the Philippines: From Indios Bravos to Filipinos*. New York: Overlook Press.
- Karnow, Stanley, 1990. *In Our Image: America's Empire in the Philippines*. New York: Ballantine Books.
- Jagor, Fedor, 1875. *Travels in the Philippines*. 2002 Edition. Boston: Adamant Media Corporation.
- Laya, Jaime C. & Gatbonton, Esperanza B., 1983. *Intramuros of Memory*. Manila: Ministry of Human Settlements, Intramuros Administration.
- Rizal, José P., 1887. *Touch Me Not (Noli Mi Tangere)*. New York: Penguin Classics.
- Romulo, Beth Day, 1976. *Manila Hotel*. Diamond Jubilee Edition. Manila: Manila Hotel.
- Torres, Jose Victor Z., 2005. *Ciudad Murada – A Walk Through Historic Intramuros*. Manila: Intramuros Administration and Vibal Publishing House.
- Zaide, Gregorio F. and Zaide, Sonia M., 1999. *Jose Rizal – Life, Works and Writings of a Genius, Writer, Scientist and National Hero*. Quezon City: All Nations Publishing Co., Inc.
- Zaragoza, Ramon Ma., 1990. *Old Manila*. Singapore: Oxford University Press.

Hong Kong

- Coward, Sir Noel, 1932. "Mad Dogs and Englishmen." New York.
- Han, Suyin, 1952. *A Many Splendoured Thing*. UK: Johnathan Cape.
- Hibbard, Peter, 2010. *Beyond Hospitality – The History of the Hongkong and Shanghai Hotels, Limited*. Singapore: Marshall-Cavendish Editions.
- Ingham, Michael, 2007. *Hong Kong – A Cultural and Literary History*. Oxford: Signal Books.
- Lee, Leo Ou-Fan, 2008. *City Between Worlds – My Hong Kong*. USA: The Belknapp Press of Harvard University Press.
- McDonogh, Gary and Wong, Cindy, 2005. *Global Hong Kong*. New York: Routledge.
- Ng, Maria N., 2009. *Pilgrimages: Memories of Colonial Macau and Hong Kong*. Hong Kong: Hong Kong University Press.
- Sandhaus, Derek, 2010. *Tales of Old Hong Kong – Treasures from the Fragrant Harbour*. Hong Kong: Earnshaw Books.

Picture Credits

All photography, maps, prints, postcards and other archival material are the author's except where listed below.

The author and publisher would like to thank the following individuals, museums and hotels for their contribution towards the telling of this tale of travel in South East Asia. Every possible effort has been made to identify, locate and contact owners of copyright and to seek formal permission for reproducing these images.

Collection of the British Library. Page 33 (top)

Courtesy of H. Lin Ho. Page 67 (bottom)

Courtesy of Hotel Continental, Ho Chi Minh City. Pages 140 (left), 141 (inset)

Courtesy of Hotel Majapahit, Surabaya. Pages 112, 114 (middle), 115 (top)

Courtesy of Hotel Majestic, Ho Chi Minh City. Page 142(top), 143 (bottom right)

Courtesy of Hsien Yoong How. Pages 32 (top right), 196 (top), 203 (top right)

Courtesy of Ibamoto Takehiko. Page 28 (top left)

Collection of the Imperial War Museum, London. Page 109 (bottom left)

Courtesy of John Koh. Pages 8, 9 (bottom left), 10 (all), 12, 13 (all except bottom left), 15 (right), 29 (bottom left, bottom middle, and bottom right), 42 (top right), 50 (left), 73 (bottom right), 98 (bottom middle), 101 (bottom left), 120 (left), 133 (bottom left and bottom right), 136 (right bottom), 138 (top right), 140 (top), 146 (left), 150 (top), 151 (top left and bottom right), 155 (bottom right), 159 (bottom), 163 (right), 175 (right), 181 (bottom right), 182 (left), 183 (bottom right), 186 (bottom left)

Courtesy of Koh Seow Chuan. Pages 1, 133 (top right), 151 (top right and bottom left), 173 (inset)

Courtesy of Jacker Lau. Page 85 (left)

Courtesy of The Majestic Malacca. Page 69

Courtesy of Manila Hotel. Page 187 (inset)

Courtesy of Mandarin Oriental, Bangkok. Pages 119 (right), 128, 129 (bottom left)

Courtesy of Emily Marcar & the late Arshak Sarkies, via Ilsa Sharp, Perth, Western Australia (author, 'There Is Only One Raffles', Souvenir Press, London 1981/1986 – Souvenir Press Ltd, London, 1st edition ISBN 0 285 62383 4, and 2nd edition ISBN: 0 285 62744 9). Pg 15 (left).

Courtesy of Herbridge Mo. Page 190 (bottom left)

Courtesy of the National Museum of Singapore, National Heritage Board. Pages 14 (left), 32 (right bottom), 44 (top left), 54, 56 (right), 58 (top left), 58 (right), 60 (bottom left), 61 (top left), 65 (top left and top right), 66 (bottom left), 70, 74 (top), 75 (left), 79 (left)

Collection of the National Portrait Gallery, London. Page 73 (top right)

Courtesy of John Nicholson. Pages 100 (left), 129 (bottom right)

Courtesy of The Peninsula Hotel, Hong Kong. Pages 202, 203 (top left and top middle, bottom right), 204, 205

Courtesy of Ronnie Pinsler. Pages 40, 41 (bottom left), 42 (top left), 43 (inset), 45 (right bottom), 48 (bottom left), 49 (top)

Courtesy of Ian Pringle. Pages 21 (right), 188

Courtesy of a private collector. Page 123 (bottom right)

Courtesy of Raffles Hotel Le Royal, Phnom Penh. Pages 157, 158 (top right)

Courtesy of Raffles Hotel, Singapore. Page 87 (top), 88 (left), 89 (bottom left)

Courtesy of Rahim bin Kassim. Page 147 (top)

Courtesy of Sofitel Legend Metropole Hanoi. Pages 172 (top), 173 (top), 174 (top)

Courtesy of Su Tho Pei Pei. Page 47 (left)

Courtesy of Amnah Tan. Page 62 (bottom right, top and bottom)

Courtesy of Joe Tan. Page 46 (bottom right)

Courtesy of Tan Yu Huat. Pages 191 (inset), 192 (bottom left), 193 (bottom right), 194 (top)

Courtesy of Jacob Termansen. Pages 47 (in box bottom right), 51 (left), 53 (right and bottom left), 57 (inset) , 59 (bottom left, bottom middle, bottom right), 63 (left), 67 (top left and top middle), 68

Courtesy of Luca Invernizzi Tettoni. Pages 2, 22, 23 (bottom left), 24 (top left), 25 (top left), 27 (inset), 28 (bottom right), 31, 33 (bottom inset), 34 (top left), 35 (bottom left and left), 46 (top right), 47 (in box top and bottom left), 59 (far right bottom), 71 (top), 76 (left top and left bottom), 77 (top), 78 (inset), 79 (right), 80, 81, 82 (inset), 83 (top middle left, top middle right, top right), 85, 86 (left), 88 (top right, bottom middle, and bottom right), 89 (top), 116, 118 (bottom right), 121 (top), 122 (top left and top right), 124 (top), 125 (right top and bottom), 126 (top left and right), 127 (bottom right), 133 (left), 134 (inset), 135 (bottom inset), 136 (inset), 139 (top right, middle left and middle right), 152 (left bottom), 153 (top left), 154 (all), 155 (background), 163 (left), 165 (top), 166 (top), 167 (top left), 169 (top left, bottom left, right middle), 171 (left, right third from top), 172 (top left)

Courtesy of Alan Tow. Pages 84 (bottom right), 85 (top right), 165 (bottom right)

Courtesy of Jan Veenendahl. Page 95 (top)

Images in the Public Domain

Page 22 (bottom left), 24 (top right), 34 (bottom right), 56 (left), 65 (bottom), 111 (bottom left and all at bottom right), 123 (top right), 158 (bottom), 185 (top right), Page 198 (bottom right)

Copyright Free Images

Page 76 (bottom)

Images from Creative Commons

Page 30 – By Esme Vos, "Inside the Musmeah Yeshua Synagogue," licensed under the Creative Commons Attribution 2.0 Generic license. http://commons.wikimedia.org/wiki/File:Musmeah_Yeshua_synagogue.jpg

Page 46 (top middle) – By Gryffindor, "Islamic Museum Penang Dec 2006 001", licensed under the Creative Commons Attribution 2.5 Generic license http://commons.wikimedia.org/wiki/File:Islamic_Museum_Penang_Dec_2006_001.jpg

Page 93 (bottom left) – By Heaven's Army, "Borobudur 2008", licensed under the Creative Commons Attribution 3.0 Unported license. http://commons.wikimedia.org/wiki/File:Borobudur_2008.JPG

Page 93 (bottom right) – By Brigitte Werner, "Mount Merapi and 6 other Volcanoes in Java", licensed under the Creative Commons CC0 1.0 Universal Public Domain Dedication license. http://commons.wikimedia.org/wiki/File:Merapi_and_6_other_ Volcanoes_in_Java_Indonesia.jpg

Page 137 (bottom right) – By Jean-Pierre Dalbéra, "Temple taoïste de Thiên Hâu (Hô Chi Minh-Ville) (6697749441)", licensed under the Creative Commons Attribution 2.0 Generic License. http://commons.wikimedia.org/wiki/File:Temple_tao%C3%AFste_de_Thi%C3%AAn_H%E1%BA%ADu_(H%C3%B4_Chi_Minh-Ville)_(6697749441).jpg

Page 139 (bottom) – By La_Pluie_d'été_au_Stella.jpg: Jutta Johanna, "Marguerite Duras 1993", licensed under the Creative Commons Attribution 3.0 Unported license. http://commons.wikimedia.org/wiki/File:Marguerite_Duras_1993.jpg

Page 148 (top right) – By Werner.pauwels, "Cambodia, Phnom Penh, Royal Palace as seen from acros Tonle Sap River", licensed under Creative Commons Attribution 3.0 Unported license. http://commons.wikimedia.org/wiki/File:Cambodia,_Phnom_Penh,_Royal_Palace_as_seen_from_acros_Tonle_Sap_River.jpg

Page 163 – By Chinasaur, "Flag tower, Hanoi", licensed under the Creative Commons Attribution-Share Alike 2.0 Generic license. http://commons.wikimedia.org/wiki/File:Flag_tower,_Hanoi.jpg

Page 183 (inset) – By Toby Roca, "Late afternoon in Escolta 2", licensed under the Creative Commons Attribution-Share Alike 3.0 Unported license. http://commons.wikimedia.org/wiki/File:Late_afternoon_in_Escolta_2.JPG

Page 185 (bottom left) – By SeamanWell, "PhillipinePostOffice", licensed under Creative Commons Attribution-Share Alike 3.0 Unported. http://commons.wikimedia.org/wiki/File:PhilippinePostOffice.JPG

Page 194 (right middle) – http://hkrail.wikia.com/wiki/檔案:Peak_Tram_Appearance.JPG

Page 197 (top) – By MingHong, "Happy Valley 1", licensed under Creative Commons Attribution-Share Alike 4.0 International, 3.0 Unported, 2.5 Generic, 2.0 Generic and 1.0 Generic license. http://commons.wikimedia.org/wiki/File:Happy_Valley_1.jpg